You hold in your hand a book that will bless your life. On any religious subject there are scores of books, but often one rises far above all others on a vital Bible topic. I now have my copy of what I consider the definitive book standing above others on this topic. As you read this book you will see how the author combines two charges Paul gives to preachers. "Preach the word" and "The servant of the Lord must not quarrel but be gentle to all ... in humility correcting those who are in opposition." Those who sincerely believe there can be only one literal cup in the Lord's supper, and who read this book, will find a teacher with a compassionate heart seeking to help us all understand God's will. This book is a masterpiece. It stands high above all other books on this topic.

- **Dan Jenkins**, Evangelist
Palm Beach Gardens, FL

This book guides the reader to examine the subject and solution to these matters which have divided the brethren for too long. It is my hope that this excellent, extensive, and exhaustive study will bring the unity for which our Lord prayed (John 17), and the unity that the Holy Spirit planned (Ephesians 4). Paul plead for unity (1 Corinthians 1:10). To be divided is to ignore the prayer, the plan, and the plea.

This book provides the reader with sound doctrine that cannot be condemned (Titus 2:8). The study of this subject is clear, concise, and complete. The author used the tools of biblical understanding (Psalm 119:130). He handled the word rightly (2 Timothy 2:15). He gathered the scriptures on the subject (Isaiah 28:9-13). It is my prayer that the readers of this book will be noble and search the scriptures (Acts 17:11), and become doers of the word (James 2:22).

- **David Meek**, Evangelist
Lebanon, TN

Brethren and friends; the volume you now hold in your hands, sets out in clear and unmistakable terms, the truth about the Anti (Non-Institutional) "One cup" position. It is a scholarly treatise of an issue that has divided the Lord's church for decades. It is written in love, with the souls of men in view. The goal of this book is to teach truth and restore unity.

This volume treats those who may disagree with the utmost respect, and seeks restoration based upon the Bible. The Bible demands us to follow the pattern of sound words regarding things spiritual and in all of life (II Tim. 1:13; Heb. 8:5). Douglas E. Dingley has met that demand in this volume. This book earnestly contends for the faith (Jude 3). Between the covers you will find each argument in favor of binding the "One cup" issue, answered fully and in love. The author has very carefully avoided personal attacks and ascribing to them positions they do not hold. This is a "No straw man" book and will richly bless all who read its pages.

I have personally done much work and study on Non-institutionalism - and have found no greater material on this issue. I highly recommend this work. I have gladly added this great book to my library. I hope you do as well.

- **Robby Eversole**, Summerville, GA.

Clearing Up The Confusion

The Cup; The Cross; and The Chaos!

Douglas E. Dingley

James Kay Publishing

Tulsa, Oklahoma

Clearing Up The Confusion
The Cup; The Cross; and The Chaos!
ISBN 978-1-943245-25-3

www.jameskaypublishing.com
e-mail: sales@jameskaypublishing.com

© 2018 Douglas E. Dingley
Cover design by JKP

2.0
All rights reserved.
No part of this book may be reproduced
in any form or by any means
- except for review questions and brief quotations -
without permission in writing from the author.

All Scripture references taken from
the New King James Version
unless otherwise noted

Other Biblically-Sound Resources By Douglas E. Dingley

Books:

Effective Everyday Evangelism

More Than Conquerors

Both available now at:
www.jameskaypublishing.com/BookStore
&
www.amazon.com/author/douglasdingley

Articles:

http://churchofchristarticles.com/blog/category/doug-dingley

Bible Studies + Audio Sermons:

www.Godswordistruth.org

(Scannable QR Codes for Links are at the Back of this Book)

I would like to express my deepest and most sincere gratitude and appreciation to brothers Wayne Burger and Dale Jenkins for their proof-reading and pre-publication comments and contributions to this work; to sister Yvonne Conner for her constant encouragement to get published and bring this project to completion; and especially to my lovely wife and sister in Christ, Karen, for all of her love, support, patience, and sacrifice over the course of my endeavoring to produce this in-depth study which you are about to embark upon. May God richly bless all of them for their labor of love on its – and subsequently His – behalf; and may He also bless you, the reader, as you diligently read and biblically study your way through it.

Douglas E. Dingley

A Note from the Author:

The very night – and in fact, only just a few short hours - before our Lord and Savior Jesus Christ was wrongly arrested, falsely prosecuted, shamefully sentenced, brutally beaten, sickeningly scourged, and then horrifically crucified on Golgotha's cross for all of the sins and evil of all mankind throughout all generations, He celebrated the Passover and instituted that which was divinely designed to bring all of His earthly followers both unity and oneness, with both Him and one another, from the day His church would be established onward, until He returned for His faithful people.

However, it is precisely this perfectly and divinely-designed and instituted observance, the human handling, mishandling, and misunderstanding of which, has incredibly, unbelievably, and even almost inconceivably, brought about such a seemingly great and hopeless divide in the blood-bought body and bride of Christ, as to appear virtually unhealable.

But thanks be to God, that with Him all things are possible! Thanks be to God, that this ugly, ghastly, gaping, and ungodly wound need not be fatal! It is the hope, intent, and purpose of this effort, to lovingly examine this problem, and to then hopefully administer appropriate doses of the all-sufficient and biblical balm of Gilead. All of this to thus begin the long-overdue and much-needed process of healing this ugly division in His beautiful and blood-bought bride, prior to His return for her and her heavenly 'wedding day.'

As with all prescribed treatment processes for healing any such far-reaching and potentially life-threatening problems, this book is broken down into several different stages of exploration, determination, identification, and application. While its first few chapters discuss in great detail 'the call which led to it all,' they are also carefully crafted and purposely designed to provide readers from both the 'one cup' as well as the 'multi-cup' perspectives with a comprehensive look at some of the other spiritual and scriptural 'common ground' issues which all of us as God's children who are sincerely striving to be the kind of worshippers the Father is seeking (John 4:23-24), most assuredly already agree and stand united together upon.

And then, once that foundation is firmly established, we move on into an in-depth exploration of each and every one of the actual verses in the New Testament which include the word "cup," examining them carefully in the all-illuminating light of God's holy word, thus building up both our own biblical understanding, as well as building towards a better, healthier, and more scriptural treatment plan to address and alleviate the problem.

Then, lastly, we move on to a biblically-sound, common ground conclusion, which I believe to be the complete and final cure for this otherwise life-threatening and ghastly division in the beloved and blood-bought body and bride of Christ.

I am extremely excited and confident in Christ Jesus, that for those who would honestly, objectively, and sincerely study through these chapters with an open Bible and an open and humble heart before God (Isaiah 66:1-2), that we can all come to the one, same, common, and Christ-desired conclusion (Ephesians 4:1-6; Philippians 1:27-2:2).

It is to this end that I have written. It is to this end that I have striven. And it is to this end and effort that I hope and pray that our Lord God will give His most holy and peace-bringing blessing. And for whatever good and/or heavenly healing that might ever result from this humble effort: To God be all the glory – always and in all ways. Or, as our divinely-inspired brother and the apostle Paul wrote so long ago in God's epistle to the first-century congregation of the church of Christ which worked and worshipped together in Ephesus: "Now to Him who is able to do exceedingly abundantly above all that we ask or think, according to the power that works in us, to Him be glory in the church by Christ Jesus to all generations forever and ever. Amen." (Ephesians 3:20-21).

Table of Contents

A Note from the Author: xi

1. The Call 1

2. The Conviction 13

3. The Calamity 23

4. The Conceptualization 37

5. The Confusion (Part One) 49

6. The Confusion (Part Two) 61

7. The Cup (Considered) 73

8. The Communion 85

9. The Corinthians 103

10. The Chronicle 119

11. The Conclusions 135

12. The Crusade 149

Appendix 159

NOTES

Chapter One:

The Call

Most elders, preachers, and church office personnel will tell you that they typically field many and varied telephone calls over the course of a year. Sometimes it's telemarketers pedaling everything from electronic donation devices and services, to entertainment and sports entities seeking to give youth group discounts for their next big event, to vinyl siding and windows contractors hoping for their next large job.

Unfortunately, probably a far greater concentration of the phone calls we field come from those folks who have somehow conditioned themselves to think that the church is just a bottomless bank or some other sort of charitable entity for them to continually obtain free resources from. While some of the needs and circumstances expressed in such calls are truly legitimate, many of these calls come in from folks who will come up with any one of a vast variety of contrived, compelling, emotionally-charged but completely self-contradicting (upon closer examination) stories, all designed to score and squeeze a few more bucks out of the church. At least that is, until it is suggested that they bring the entire family to Bible study and worship services so that we can thereafter sit down and discuss their request, because after all, the church is more in the business of addressing their eternal spiritual condition and need, rather than their momentary monetary one. It has been my personal experience over the years however, that in the overwhelming majority of these cases, such people – despite the desperate nature of their described need at the beginning of such telephone calls – seldom, if ever, seem to have it bad enough to actually show up for the spiritual services the church is offering, even if it means that they might potentially get a portion of their financial needs met in some form or fashion by so doing.

However, the particular telephone call that came in as I sat in the church office that specific spring day several years ago was actually none of the above. A pleasant female voice came on the other end of the line as she identified herself and then went on to somewhat hesitantly begin to explain the purpose for her call. She was a sister in Christ from somewhere over towards the east coast who was planning to travel to Tulsa with her husband and family a little later on in the summer to attend a certain days-long event, and was subsequently calling ahead to try to find a faithful-to-the-word-of-God congregation of the Lord's church for she and her family to worship with. Very commendable – and even completely essential in today's irreverent and stormy spiritual climate I might add! Due to the sad state of affairs in the Lord's church today as some of God's own children decide to deride, deny, over-ride, disrespect, disobey, discard, and disregard the Lord's New Testament pattern[1] and authority[2] when it comes to His one and only blood-bought church[3], such calls have now, sadly become far more commonplace, and are actually considered to be pretty much of a necessity for the faithful. In fact, I've been forced to make more than one of them myself over the past few years as we and others have planned family vacations.

The fact is that fifty to sixty or so years ago when the people of God travelled, it didn't really much matter where they went; if the sign out front identified the group meeting for worship and Bible study inside on Sunday as one of the local congregations of the churches of Christ[4], then they could rest assured that the teaching and worship service that they were about to experience and participate in by attending there were almost always going to be in conformity with what the Bible taught, as well as what they had expected, experienced, and enjoyed in previous congregations of the Lord's church where they had worshipped.

This was just like in the first century A.D. after the Lord's church was established on the Day of Pentecost as recorded in Acts 2:1-47, when that same, one system of teaching - or "the

---

[1] Philippians 3:15-19; 2 Timothy 1:13; Titus 2:1-8; Hebrews 8:1-6.
[2] Matthew 28:18-20; John 17:1-3; 2 Peter 2:1-19; Jude 1:3-8.
[3] Matthew 16:18-19; Acts 20:28.
[4] Romans 16:16.

apostle's doctrine" as it was referred to (Acts 2:42) - was rigidly, reverently, and religiously taught "everywhere in every church" (1 Corinthians 4:17), or, "in all the churches" (1 Corinthians 7:17; See also: 1 Corinthians 11:16).

The first-century congregation or church of Christ in Philippi was taught to follow the same, exact, divinely-inspired pattern (Philippians 3:16-19; 2 Timothy 1:13) of doctrine (or teaching) as the first-century congregation of the Lord's faithful and blood-bought people in Corinth (1 Corinthians 16:1). The first-century congregation of the church of Christ in Colossae was taught to obey the same, exact, divinely-inspired pattern of doctrine or God-given body of teaching as the first-century congregation of the Lord's church in Laodicea - and vice-versa (Colossians 4:16).

This same, exact, divinely-inspired pattern of doctrine or system of spiritual teaching has served the faithful who wished and wanted more than anything else in the world to be the kind of worshippers the Father was seeking (John 4:23-24) very well over the past two millennia, ever since the Holy Spirit guided God's hand-picked and divinely-inspired messengers into delivering it (John 16:12-15; 2 Timothy 3:14-4:4; 2 Peter 3:1-4).

Some of these very distinctive and divinely dictated directives from almighty God Himself[5] include His express desire that the pouring out of His peoples' musical praise, devotion, and adoration to Him is the personal privilege and responsibility of each and every faithful and blood-bought member of His church. Hence, never was there ever even once seen any such thing as a specialized, 'for entertainment purposes only' choir, 'praise team,' soloist, or mechanical instrument of music found anywhere in any of His first-century churches (or congregations). Check your Bible.[6] Check your church history.[7] These vain and man-made, counter-biblical musical concepts, doctrines, and desires are totally foreign to God's instruction in the New

---

[5] 1 Peter 1:16-21.
[6] See the only eight passages in the entire New Testament wherein almighty God commands the precise type of music He wants His church on earth to give Him: Matthew 26:30; Mark 14:26; Acts 16:25; Romans 15:9; 1 Corinthians 14:15; Ephesians 5:19; Colossians 3:16; Hebrews 2:12; and James 5:13.
[7] See: "Worksheet Study – The Sin Of Offering Instrumental Music To God," under Doug's "Bible Studies" tab, at www.Godswordistruth.org.

Testament, being therefore totally useless, pointless, and worthless as far as worship pleasing to God goes today.[8]

Other elements of this divinely desired, inspired, and insisted upon doctrine delivered directly from the throne of almighty God Himself for His church for all time[9], include the timeless edict that no woman in any age is ever to teach over, have authority over, lead prayers, lead songs, or in any other way take the lead over the men in the Lord's church. It is instead, a direct command from almighty God Himself that they remain silent and in submission according to 1 Timothy 2:8-15 and 1 Corinthians 14:33-37. (Please also note that this is not a culturally-adjustable commandment, as the Lord makes it very clear in that 1 Timothy passage that this divine directive supersedes all times and cultures by taking us all the way back to the veritable beginning of creation when He originally established it. For a full and accurate biblical discourse on this subject, please see the "***Peripheral Reasoning – Women's Roles In The Church***" study, under the "Bible Studies" tab at **www.Godswordistruth.org**.)

The first-century churches of Christ also understood and practiced the same God-given, Spirit-directed, apostle-dispersed doctrine on salvation as well. And that was that repentance and baptism into Christ, specifically for the forgiveness of one's sins, was the one and only, exact and exclusive point at which one called upon the Name of the Lord and was thus saved by God's grace through their faith. Salvation was never reported as occurring in the New Testament Scriptures through simply reciting some man-made prayer. Nor was salvation ever reported therein as occurring one sadly misinformed millisecond before that biblically-required repentance and baptism for those biblically-required reasons (See: Acts 2:37-42, 22:16; Romans 6:1-23; Galatians 3:26-27; 1 Peter 3:21).

The so-called "pious unimmersed" as some might refer to them today (such as 'good' Cornelius as seen in Acts 10:1-48), were never viewed as anything more than lost sinners who needed to repent and obey the gospel by being buried with Him

---

[8] Matthew 15:1-9; Mark 7:1-13.
[9] 2 Timothy 3:1-4:4.

in that same water baptism[10], thus being saved by virtue of their being born again of both the water and the Spirit at the same time[11], no matter how 'good' or pious they previously were, prior to.

These are just a few of the eternally-bound elements[12] of the apostles' doctrine that all the congregations of the first-century church of Christ and their leadership were commanded to command and insist upon.[13] These patterns and practices were those which travelers in the first century could subsequently count on encountering when it came to their Sunday worship in any other foreign cities, lands, cultures, or countries.

And why not? The church of Christ is the body of Christ (Ephesians 1:22-23, Colossians 1:18, 24). And as the apostle Paul told the first-century congregation of that portion of the Lord's body that worked and worshipped in Ephesus, "There is one body and one Spirit, just as you were called in one hope of your calling; one Lord, one faith, one baptism, one God and Father of all, who is above all, and through all, and in you all" (Ephesians 4:4-6). One, unified, united, and spiritually undivided body of believers[14], all taking their orders from the same, one Head and only King of that body, the Lord Jesus Christ Himself (Colossians 1:15-24). No wonder there was - and is - supposed to be complete unity, community, and continuity in the Lord's one, New Testament body/church. One unified and undenominated faith, doctrine, and practice in all the congregations of Christ's church, simply because they all taught and insisted on the same exact instruction, from the same exact source – the walking and written word of God (John 17:1-21).

Conversely, any individuals and/or congregations which rebelliously and irreverently diverted from it and taught any other doctrine, gospel, or perverted versions or variations thereof, instead of the one gospel which the divinely-inspired, handpicked and Holy-Spirit driven apostles and authors of our Lord and Savior so carefully and obediently taught[15], were

---

[10] 2 Thessalonians 1:3-10; 1 Peter 4:14-17; Romans 6:1-4, 10:16-17; Colossians 2:11-12.
[11] 1 Peter 3:21; John 3:3-5; Acts 2:38.
[12] Psalm 119:89; Matthew 16:19; Revelation 22:18-19.
[13] 1 Timothy 1:3-7, 4:1-16.
[14] 1 Corinthians 1:9-10, 12:12-27; Ephesians 4:1-6.
[15] 2 Corinthians 4:2; 2 Timothy 2:15-18, 4:1-4.

summarily and completely condemned outright. In fact, if they did not repent, it was commanded that they were to be thereafter noted, marked, and avoided, according to those very same, first-century, divinely-inspired and driven writers such as the apostles Paul, Peter, and John:

- "Greet one another with a holy kiss. The churches of Christ greet you. Now I urge you, brethren, note those who cause divisions and offenses, contrary to the doctrine which you learned, and avoid them. For those who are such do not serve our Lord Jesus Christ, but their own belly, and by smooth words and flattering speech deceive the hearts of the simple" (Romans 16:16-18).

- "I marvel that you are turning away so soon from Him who called you in the grace of Christ, to a different gospel, which is not another; but there are some who trouble you and want to pervert the gospel of Christ. But even if we, or an angel from heaven, preach any other gospel to you than what we have preached to you, let him be accursed. As we have said before, so now I say again, if anyone preaches any other gospel to you than what you have received, let him be accursed. For do I now persuade men, or God? Or do I seek to please men? For if I still pleased men, I would not be a bondservant of Christ" (Galatians 1:6-10).

- "For I want you to know what a great conflict I have for you and those in Laodicea, and *for* as many as have not seen my face in the flesh, that their hearts may be encouraged, being knit together in love, and *attaining* to all riches of the full assurance of understanding, to the knowledge of the mystery of God, both of the Father and of Christ, in whom are hidden all the treasures of wisdom and knowledge. Now this I say lest anyone should deceive you with persuasive words. For though I am absent in the flesh, yet I am with you in spirit, rejoicing to see your *good* order and the steadfastness of your faith in Christ. As you have therefore received

Christ Jesus the Lord, so walk in Him, rooted and built up in Him and established in the faith, as you have been taught, abounding in it with thanksgiving. Beware lest anyone cheat you through philosophy and empty deceit, according to the tradition of men, according to the basic principles of the world, and not according to Christ. For in Him dwells all the fullness of the Godhead bodily; and you are complete in Him, who is the head of all principality and power" (Colossians 2:1-10).

- "Therefore, brethren, stand fast and hold the traditions which you were taught, whether by word or our epistle… Finally, brethren, pray for us, that the word of the Lord may run *swiftly* and be glorified, just as *it is* with you, and that we may be delivered from unreasonable and wicked men; for not all have faith. But the Lord is faithful, who will establish you and guard *you* from the evil one. And we have confidence in the Lord concerning you, both that you do and will do the things we command you. Now may the Lord direct your hearts into the love of God and into the patience of Christ. But we command you, brethren, in the name of our Lord Jesus Christ, that you withdraw from every brother who walks disorderly and not according to the tradition which he received from us… And if anyone does not obey our word in this epistle, note that person and do not keep company with him, that he may be ashamed. Yet do not count *him* as an enemy, but admonish *him* as a brother" (2 Thessalonians 2:15, 3:1-6, 14-15).

- "As I urged you when I went into Macedonia—remain in Ephesus that you may charge some that they teach no other doctrine, nor give heed to fables and endless genealogies, which cause disputes rather than godly edification which is in faith. Now the purpose of the commandment is love from a pure heart, *from* a good conscience, and *from* sincere faith, from which some, having strayed, have turned aside to idle talk, desiring to be teachers of the law, understanding neither what they say nor the things which they affirm… If anyone teaches otherwise and does not consent to wholesome words, *even* the words of our Lord Jesus Christ, and to the doctrine which accords with godliness, he is proud, knowing nothing, but is obsessed with disputes and arguments over words, from which come envy, strife, reviling, evil suspicions, useless wranglings of men of corrupt minds and destitute of the truth, who suppose that godliness is a *means of* gain. From such withdraw yourself" (1 Timothy 1:3-7; 6:2-5).

- "For we did not follow cunningly devised fables when we made known to you the power and coming of our Lord Jesus Christ, but were eyewitnesses of His majesty. For He received from God the Father honor and glory when such a voice came to Him from the Excellent Glory: 'This is My beloved Son, in whom I am well pleased.' And we heard this voice which came from heaven when we were with Him on the holy mountain. And so we have the prophetic word confirmed, which you do well to heed as a light that shines in a dark place, until the day dawns and the morning star rises in your hearts; knowing this first, that no prophecy of Scripture is of any private interpretation, for prophecy never came by the will of man, but holy men of God spoke *as they were* moved by the Holy Spirit. But there were also false prophets among the people, even as there will be false teachers among you, who will secretly bring in destructive heresies, even denying the Lord who bought them, *and* bring on themselves swift destruction. And many will follow their destructive ways, because of whom the way of truth will be blasphemed. By covetousness they will exploit you with deceptive words; for a long time their judgment has not been idle, and their destruction does not slumber" (2 Peter 1:16-2:3).

- "Whoever transgresses and does not abide in the doctrine of Christ does not have God. He who abides in the doctrine of Christ has both the Father and the Son. If anyone comes to you and does not bring this doctrine, do not receive him into your house nor greet him; for he who greets him shares in his evil deeds" (2 John 1:9-11).

The mid to late 1st century wasn't all that different from the mid to late 20th century in one respect within the Lord's one, New Testament church. Churches of Christ in both cases had initially appreciated, reverenced, loved, and obeyed their Lord and Savior by humbly and simply carrying out His commands. But then, the winds of change began to blow, as fickle mortal man in the mid to late 20th century once again did what fickle-and-unsatisfied-with-God's-perfect-plan mortal man has never gone too long without doing.[16] And along came a much less submissive, much more aggressive, proud, rebellious, selfish and more irreverent generation and movement, spearheaded by several soon-apostate colleges and universities "associated with churches of Christ," and the spiritually corrupted congregations and deviations from God's divinely-inspired instructions which they have so willingly helped to create. In some of those congregations wherein Satan's wolves in sheep's clothing have today taken over complete control, they have driven the entire and lemming-like flock off of the "old paths"[17] of God's straight and narrow[18] highway of holiness[19], and out onto the hellishly wide path to eternal destruction with their complete support and blessing. (Please see and study 2 Peter, Chapters 2 and 3.)

It is to the point today, that if I may illustrate by borrowing and paraphrasing some phraseology from the apostle Paul (as seen in Romans 9:6-7): "But it is not that the word of God has taken no effect. For they *are* not all church of Christ who are church of Christ, nor are they all children of God simply because they have a sign out front of their building or a website on the internet which reads 'church of Christ.'"

In other words, it takes far more than a simple claim, a colorful sign, or a wonderfully designed website that sports the designation 'church of Christ,' to honestly constitute a true and biblical, approved and accepted by God, Holy-Spirit designed

---

[16] Acts 7:9-53.
[17] Jeremiah 6:16-19.
[18] Matthew 7:13-15.
[19] Isaiah 35:8-10.

and patterned, Christ-honoring and obedient, local congregation of God's people or 'church of Christ.' As the old adage goes: "If you call a horse's tail a leg, how many legs does a horse have? Answer: Four. Reason? Because no matter what you may choose to pin on it for a name, a tail is still not a leg no matter what you may otherwise choose to arbitrarily or falsely call it." Or more simply put: It takes far more than just referring to a congregation as a 'church of Christ,' to truly and biblically make it one (Luke 6:46).

Look at it this way: The Bible is God's divine dictionary, defining and describing in definitive detail all things spiritual, just as God wants, expects, designed, desires, and demands them to be. From Acts, Chapter Two, where the Lord's church was established and brought into existence (capping off and making known the "eternal purpose which He accomplished in Christ Jesus our Lord" – See Ephesians 3:10-11), all the way through to the end of the book of Jude, is found God's very lengthy, very detailed, and very definitive depiction, description, and definition, of exactly what His Son's church is, practices, and looks like (as partially described in the doctrinal discussion above). Therefore, it just naturally follows, that any church, either in the first, twenty-first, and/or any other century in between or to come afterwards (Lord willing), which neither fits nor conforms to His concise definition of what His Son's church is, looks, and worships like, simply isn't His Son's church or body of saved people according to God's word. This, no matter what their humanly-devised wisdom, website, leadership, or sign out front might possibly proclaim (Romans 3:4; 2 Thessalonians 2:9-14).

Understanding that divinely-inspired dynamic completely, as this good sister from over towards the east coast very gently and respectfully approached the subjects at hand that May day, I, having also understood after only a few brief moments the nature and purpose of her telephone call, decided to 'cut right to the chase' as it were, and save her some time and potential discomfort. I wanted to immediately ease her mind and let her know right up front that we were indeed a faithful to the old paths, God-fearing, Jesus-loving, Bible believing, and Scripture respecting, obeying, and practicing congregation of Christ's church (Romans 16:16).

"Let me help you out," I said. I went on to assure her that if she and her family came to worship with us, they would not need to worry about experiencing vain worship conducted according to the desires, doctrines, and deceptions of men (Mark 7:1-13), but would be amongst humble brethren in Christ, worshipping in spirit and truth, and hence seeking with all their hearts, souls, minds, and strength, to be exactly the kind of worshippers the Father is always seeking, according to His word (John 4:23-24). As a result, her family would certainly never encounter such biblically-contradictory doctrines and practices as females leading songs, leading prayers, preaching sermons, or serving in leadership roles of any sort – such as on the Lord's table or possibly as a part of some thinly-disguised but still song-leading, leadership-positioned 'praise team'- in direct violation of the Lord's divinely-inspired instructions and commandments in places like 1 Corinthians 14:33-37 and 1 Timothy 2:11-15. And that furthermore, it would be harder to find a musical instrument in our building than it is to find the so-called 'sinner's prayer of faith for salvation' in the Scriptures – absolutely non-existent in both cases.

At that point - although she seemed pleased thus far - she went on to ask if we observed communion each first day of the week (which of course we do - once again in loving obedience and accordance with the Lord's divinely-dictated pattern and example as well – Acts 20:7). And it was then that she finally got around and down to it. The question, concern, and conviction that shall be discussed at length in the very next chapter…

NOTES

Chapter Two:

The Conviction

After the discussion of our congregation's worship service elements as explored in Chapter One, this good sister then respectfully inquired as to whether we as a congregation all drank from the same, one, lone communion cup, or, if we divided the fruit of the vine down into multiple communion containers before partaking. I responded that we used multiple containers for the fruit of the vine which we drank during communion. She then went on to reveal how she and her husband were members of a 'one cup' congregation and related how fruitlessly to this point she had searched to find one in Oklahoma for her family to worship with. The last time they had been in Tulsa she said they had travelled for five hours, ***one way***, to worship with a 'one-cup' congregation in Arkansas. What incredible strength of conviction I thought! I mean, can you even begin to imagine travelling for some five hours or more, past countless congregations that simply use multiple individual communion cups, just to walk into a congregation full of total strangers, specifically to all drink from the same, one cup? I certainly admired this good sister's courage and strength of conviction to say the least.

But, here's the thing that everyone needs to know and to be totally and completely aware of at all times when it comes to all matters religious, spiritual, and eternal:

It is not the <u>strength</u> of one's conviction, that determines the <u>correctness</u> of that conviction!

For the sake of your eternal soul, please take just a moment right now to really process, digest, and truly internalize that one, vital, all-important eternal truth: It is not the strength of one's convictions, that automatically determines the correctness of those convictions. How much we need to get this! It is not the firmness with which one holds to, lives out, and/or exhibits their beliefs, that necessarily correlates with, or indicates to any degree, the level of truth or God-approved content contained within those same, deeply defined and defended convictions. And it does not matter whether we're talking about yours, mine, hers, or anyone else's; whether the pope's, the pastor's, our parents, or any other religious persons. Some of the strongest and seemingly most spiritually mature religious people to have ever walked the face of this planet – people who would, and in some cases actually did and were happily willing to die for their convictions – were absolutely and completely dead wrong according to God's word. More than a few of them were far more than just simply mistaken; they were actually aligned, working, and warring against God, despite their absolutely rock-solid, immutable, and immovable beliefs and convictions to the contrary.

How can that happen? How is that even remotely possible? Here's how. Who, or what, would you identify as being the single, most deceptive element on the entire planet? Lawyers? Judges? Politicians? Preachers? Advertisers? Ad campaigns? Ex-spouses? Satan? Treaties? Contracts? Dreams? Hollywood actors? Who? What?

Actually, it doesn't really matter what or whom you or I would identify as the single most deceptive element on the entire planet; the only thing that truly matters is whom or what God identifies it as being. After all, God knows best.[20] And He knows far better as our Creator than any of us as His created beings do, exactly what the single most deceptive element on the entire planet is. So, what did He say? Simply this: "The heart is deceitful above all things, and desperately sick…" (Jeremiah 17:9). And there you have it.

This is why the strength of one's convictions, does not necessarily correlate on any level, into any semblance of the correctness of those same convictions according to God – no matter how long or strongly held, clutched, believed, or beloved they may be. This is why feelings, emotions, consciences, and/or previously-arrived at conclusions or

---

[20] 1 Corinthians 1:18-31.

convictions can never be considered as a completely fail-safe guide in determining whether something is actually right or wrong before almighty God. If it feels right, seems right, or looks right, doesn't mean much of anything at all in actually determining whether or not something really is right in God's all-seeing and exclusively righteousness-determining eyes.

Remember how "good," "pleasant," "desirable" and delicious the forbidden fruit looked to Eve in the Garden of Eden (Genesis 3:6)? Remember what happened when she decided to 'follow her heart' instead of her Creator's command? The same thing that happens today whenever a female proudly decides to 'follow her heart' instead of humbly obeying her Creator's command and seeks to become a preacher or preaching intern in the Lord's church.

"There is a way that seems right to a man, but its end is the way of death," King Solomon said.[21] And while I certainly admired this good sister's compelling STRENGTH of conviction in travelling five hours one way to worship with a 'one cup' group, I am, at the same time, reminded of many examples – both biblical as well as contemporary – which at times cause me to question even my own strongly-held convictions and conclusions and then go back and seek to objectively re-examine them. This, because none of us – myself included – can afford to be wrong before God, no matter how much we may think, feel, or believe we're right. Please consider with me, a few examples of this vital and essential eternal truth, as viewed through the eyes and word of God.

In Genesis 37 we have the history of Jacob. By the end of the chapter, he has become utterly and completely convinced that his beloved son Joseph has been killed by a wild beast. But despite his deepest, strongest, and most concrete of convictions and conclusions, he was wrong – dead wrong...

> "So they [*Joseph's brothers, after selling him into slavery*] took Joseph's tunic, killed a kid of the goats, and dipped the tunic in the blood. Then they sent the tunic of *many* colors, and they

---

[21] Proverbs 14:12, 16:25.

> brought *it* to their father and said, 'We have found this. Do you know whether it *is* your son's tunic or not?' And he recognized it and said, '*It is* my son's tunic. A wild beast has devoured him. **Without doubt** Joseph is torn to pieces.' Then Jacob tore his clothes, put sackcloth on his waist, and mourned for his son many days. And all his sons and all his daughters arose to comfort him; but he refused to be comforted, and he said, 'For I shall go down into the grave to my son in mourning.' Thus his father wept for him. Now the Midianites had sold him in Egypt to Potiphar, an officer of Pharaoh *and* captain of the guard" (Verses 31-36; ***emphasis*** mine - DED).

King Saul was Israel's first king. As king, he had abundant authority. However, as he was not God's prophet, there were also certain things which he very definitely did not have the authority or blessing from God to introduce, institute, or initiate as well. In 1 Samuel, Chapter 10 and verse 8, Samuel, the prophet of God, very clearly informs King Saul of upcoming events and instructs him what God wants his part in them to be. It is not a difficult instruction to understand, comprehend, or carry out. Samuel told King Saul straight up: "You shall go down before me to Gilgal; and **surely** I will come down to you to offer burnt offerings and make sacrifices of peace offerings… Seven days you shall wait, till I come to you and show you what you should do" (***emphasis*** mine - DED). So; what did Saul do? Let's take a look and see:

> "Then the Philistines gathered together to fight with Israel, thirty thousand chariots and six thousand horsemen, and people as the sand which *is* on the seashore in multitude. And they came up and encamped in Michmash, to the east of Beth Aven. When the men of Israel saw that they were in danger (for the people were distressed), then the people hid in caves, in thickets, in rocks, in holes, and in pits. And *some of* the Hebrews crossed over the Jordan to the land of Gad and

Gilead. As for Saul, he *was* still in Gilgal, and all the people followed him trembling. Then he waited seven days, according to the time set by Samuel. But Samuel did not come to Gilgal; and the people were scattered from him. So Saul said, 'Bring a burnt offering and peace offerings here to me.' And he offered the burnt offering. Now it happened, as soon as he had finished presenting the burnt offering, that Samuel came; and Saul went out to meet him, that he might greet him. And Samuel said, 'What have you done?' And Saul said, 'When I saw that the people were scattered from me, and *that* you did not come within the days appointed, and *that* the Philistines gathered together at Michmash, then I said, "The Philistines will now come down on me at Gilgal, and I have not made supplication to the LORD." Therefore I felt compelled, and offered a burnt offering.' And Samuel said to Saul, 'You have done foolishly. You have not kept the commandment of the LORD your God, which He commanded you. For now the LORD would have established your kingdom over Israel forever. But now your kingdom shall not continue. The LORD has sought for Himself a man after His own heart, and the LORD has commanded him *to be* commander over His people, because you have not kept what the LORD commanded you'" (1 Samuel 13:5-14).

Did you see it? Despite the crystal-clear, prophet-delivered, and all-authoritative commandment of God, when the going got tough, King Saul, '***FELT COMPELLED,***' and instead of staying faithful and obedient to God's command, very "*foolishly*" did that which he was very definitely not authorized by God to do. In fact, he ***felt so compelled***, that he immediately set about seeking to try to excuse and justify his heart-felt and feelings-driven act of direct defiance, disrespect, dishonor, and disobedience to God.

This became the same self-deceived and chosen pattern of impenitent behavior by King Saul which would eventually wind up costing him both the kingdom, as well as his relationship with almighty God (1 Samuel 15 and following). But alas, this is exactly what happens whenever any person (and even a king, elder, preacher, or any other leader over God's people mind you) decides to foolishly and fatally follow the dictates and desires of their own self-deceived heart and feelings, instead of faithfully following the truth of God's word - no matter how incredibly strong or completely compelling those feelings or convictions might be at the time.[22]

Consider additionally, the "great sin" of King Jeroboam. He also very foolishly and fatally followed the feelings, conclusions, convictions, and dictates and desires of his own self-justified but still-deceived heart when it came to instituting and insisting upon somewhat similar, but still unauthorized religious practices in the worship of almighty God (See: 1 Kings 12:25-33, 13:33-34; 2 Kings 17:1-23).

These examples are no different, less serious, or less disastrous, than is the case with those self-deceived and deluded leaders of God's people today[23], who have, 'after some years of devoted prayer and study,' decided to disrespect and disobey the direct command of their almighty God and Creator, by thus now justifying and insisting upon their new found 'freedom' to appoint women to leadership roles in the Lord's church. This, in direct defiance of God's all-encompassing authority and all-authoritative command (1 Corinthians 14:33-37).

And, while some Christians in some congregations may be totally and completely comfortable with such sinful and biblically-defiant conclusions, that in no way translates into said convictions being correct in any way, shape, or form before almighty God. Only by being in complete conformity, submission, and obedience to God's all-authoritative word, can one be completely assured of their worship, therefore, being absolutely and completely acceptable to Him (Mark 7:5-13; Luke 6:46; John 4:23-24, 12:48-50, 17:17).

Please also consider a few vital examples from the New Testament with me as well; examples wherein the **strength** of

---

[22] See: Jeremiah 7:16-34, 9:11-16; 11:6-11, 13:1-10, 16:10-13, 18:11-18, and 23:7-32!
[23] 2 Thessalonians 2:9-12.

one's convictions, is shown to be no indicator whatsoever, of the ***correctness*** of those same convictions as far as God is concerned. For instance, in John 11:47-53, after Jesus had proven His divinity by raising four-days-dead Lazarus, the chief priests and Pharisees called a council meeting and convinced all present that they should put Jesus to death. Did you get that? Their convictions were so strong that they were willing to kill for them. And not just Jesus, but the previously and once-dead Lazarus as well (John 12:10-11).

Nor was this the only instance in the New Testament wherein we see some incredibly religious people whose convictions were so strong – although at the same time so stunningly and completely dead wrong as to defy the imagination – that they were willing to kill for them either. In John 16:2, Jesus explained to His apostles the very night before He Himself was to be put to death at the behest of some of the most deeply convicted, devoutly religious, but still desperately self-deceived and God-rejecting people of His day, "The time is coming that whoever kills you will think that he offers God service." These people's convictions were so strong they would kill for them. But were they correct? Hardly.

In fact, Saul of Tarsus, one of the mightiest, most zealous, and most well-trained and intelligent religious men and minds of the entire first century was amongst those whose religious convictions were so incredibly strong that he would not only in his early years make a life out of wrongly persecuting Christ's first-century followers, but would actually exhaust all efforts to outright eradicate them. Yes, he too, very much like this good sister who called me, not only held religious convictions strong enough to travel great distances to carry out, but further, to literally kill over.

However, even there we see once again that the immense and overwhelming strength of such 'killer convictions' in no way changed the fact that those very same religious convictions were utterly, completely, and absolutely wrong – dead wrong. Listen to his own words years later, when he, as a now grace-cleansed and forgiven, blood-bought New Testament Christian and the apostle Paul, would revisit his previously-believed, but completely erroneous and unrighteous conclusions and convictions regarding religion:

"I am indeed a Jew, born in Tarsus of Cilicia, but brought up in this city at the feet of Gamaliel, taught according to the strictness of our fathers' law, and was zealous toward God as you all are today. I persecuted this Way to the death, binding and delivering into prisons both men and women, as also the high priest bears me witness, and all the council of the elders, from whom I also received letters to the brethren, and went to Damascus to bring in chains even those who were there to Jerusalem to be punished" (Acts 22:3-5).

"My manner of life from my youth, which was spent from the beginning among my own nation at Jerusalem, all the Jews know. They knew me from the first, if they were willing to testify, that according to the strictest sect of our religion I lived a Pharisee... Indeed, **I myself thought** I must do many things contrary to the name of Jesus of Nazareth. This I also did in Jerusalem, and many of the saints I shut up in prison, having received authority from the chief priests; and when they were put to death, I cast my vote against *them*. And I punished them often in every synagogue and compelled *them* to blaspheme; and being exceedingly enraged against them, I persecuted *them* even to foreign cities" (Acts 26:4-11; ***emphasis*** mine - DED).

We could also go back and examine human history after the first century Scriptures were completed and find countless examples of this same truth; i.e., that the strength of one's convictions, in no way indicates or translates into the correctness of those convictions according to God. But we need not go back even that far. For example, since as recently as September 11th, 2001, when a handful of cowardly, suicidal, religious terrorists skyjacked four huge passenger airliners in an effort to kill both themselves as well as thousands of defenseless men, women, and children on American soil, many other, similar, suicidal terrorist attacks have taken place all over the world. These have been conducted by those who obviously had such incredibly strong convictions that they were willing to both kill and be killed for them. Does that level of conviction mean those convictions were and/or are therefore correct before an almighty and all-loving God? Absolutely not (Proverbs 6:12-19; Matthew 5:7-9, 43-48; John 14:6; Romans 12:9-21; etc.).

But most of us don't have to go even that far back or away in order to find this same truth sadly played out repeatedly. Probably all of us have experienced hearing a knock on our door some sunny summer day past, and opened it up to find several members (and perhaps even a couple of "teen or twenty-something" year-old, unmarried "elders" – See, and compare https://en.wikipedia.org/wiki/Elder_(Latter_Day_Saints) to: 1 Timothy 3:1-7 and Titus 1:5-9) of a particular religious cult standing there. Not only are such convicted enough of their religious beliefs and conclusions to actually travel miles and miles themselves, going door-to-door (on foot no less) to share them, but in many cases, may have spent - or been in the middle of spending right then – a couple of years in training largely at their own expense.[24] Talk about strength of conviction! But alas, sadly – tragically - anyone believing in and bringing a different gospel, doctrine, or teaching than the first century apostles did[25]; or "another revelation of Jesus Christ" which is claimed to have come along approximately 1700 years after "the faith which was once for all delivered to the saints" just prior to the end of the first century[26], prove conclusively that their strength of conviction, once again, in no way equates, translates into, or proves to be necessarily indicative of, the biblical *correctness* of those very same convictions.[27]

How is it even possible to be so strongly convicted that one can utterly reject outright, what God has said in simple and easy to read black and white, regarding how to be saved, how to live, how to worship, which church is His, and basically all things religious which He has commanded in His New Testament, and then to honestly still think that God is pleased enough with

---

[24] "LDS Mission Cost," Mormon Mission Prep, last modified June 25, 2009, https://mormonmissionprep.com/preparing-for-a-mission/lds-mission-cost/.
[25] Galatians 1:6-10.
[26] Jude 3.
[27] 2 Thessalonians 2:13-17; Colossians 1:16-18.

that person (who has rejected almost everything God ever said, in favor of their own desires, conclusions, and convictions), to consider them sinless and take them to heaven? Such reasoning defies the imagination, doesn't it?

We know *how* it happens – Jeremiah 17:9; Proverbs 14:12, 16:25. And we know *that* it happens – Matthew 7:21-27. And we know that this should therefore, once and for all, unequivocally prove to all of us: **It is not the *strength* of one's convictions, that determines the *correctness* of those convictions! But it is only the "book, chapter, and verse," divinely-inspired and forever settled in heaven instructions of almighty God Himself, taken in their entirety and context, that determines the true correctness of ANYONE'S and EVERYONE'S convictions!**

Yes, a five-hour drive one way, just to drink the fruit of the vine from one communion container instead of several, is an incredibly respectable *strength* of conviction. But that, in and of itself, doesn't automatically or necessarily translate into that person's convictions being biblically correct – or incorrect for that matter. It simply signals a great *strength* of conviction. And as we've seen, biblically incorrect convictions and conclusions can be every inch and iota as strong as biblically-correct ones… can't they?

Chapter Three:

The Calamity

As we continued to chat amicably, at some point in the conversation (although I don't remember exactly when chronologically) I inquired of her if this 'one cup' vs. 'multiple communion containers' question was something which she and her husband might possibly be interested in having a long-distance Bible study with me regarding – an offer which she very politely, but very quickly, firmly, and frankly rejected.

During the course of our conversation I eventually informed her that I had a churches of Christ directory there in the office which had abbreviations indicating the several different kinds of congregations listed, including the type she was searching for. I further stated that although we were not a 'one cup' congregation, I would certainly help her to locate one for she and her family to worship with. After several more minutes of very pleasant conversation and supplying this good sister with the contact information for at least four such congregations with similar convictions in and/or around Tulsa, we concluded the phone call with her thanking me for being so 'helpful' and voicing how she wished she and her husband could worship with us. So did I.

After I hung up the phone, I was suddenly very saddened. Saddened that this good sister and her family could not be comfortable worshipping with us here. Further saddened that there are so many thousands of brethren out there who consider the use of multiple communion cups as opposed to one, to be the full and final test of faithfulness and fellowship for God's one New Testament people. Saddened that some of my very own beloved brethren in Christ can seem to somehow believe that those of the rest of us washed in the same blood, having obeyed the same gospel, having been purchased at the same price, and having been made members and ministers of the same church as they were, will somehow be spending eternity in hell simply because we use multiple communion cups to contain the fruit of the vine from which we drink during communion, instead of succumbing to their personal perspective, conviction, conclusion and insistence on everyone's using only one.

Please don't get me wrong; if the 'one cup' perspective was a biblically-accurate and scripturally-sustainable and defensible one, then I would also be all for it and would defend it to the death. But from everything I've ever seen, read, heard, or studied - and with all due respect, humility, love, and objectivity towards my beloved 'one cup' brethren - as we shall surely see in this study, it is none of the above.

I was further deeply saddened as I considered the fact that we have now, apparently, come to such a terrible place in the history of the Lord's one New Testament church, that the current publishers[28] of the so-called *Churches of Christ in the United States* directory which we have a copy of here in the church building office, feel that they have to list so many factions, fractions, divisions, separations, and abbreviations relative to who we - who are supposed to be the one, undivided, undenominated, and unified body or church of Jesus Christ (John 17:20-23; 1 Corinthians 1:10-13; Ephesians 4:4-6; Philippians 1:27) - have now become.

Take for example the "Congregational Data Confirmation Form" which I recently received from them (relative to and in advance of their new 2018 edition) which they use to gather and organize congregational information. On the back side of the form, in the "Congregational Character Codes" section, there was a very separate and distinct division entitled *"NON-INSTITUTIONAL,"* under which were found the following nine sub-divisions of the larger, overall, umbrella-type division of our beloved brotherhood usually referred to as the 'non-institutional' or 'anti' portion/section thereof:

NI - Non-institutional: oppose church support of institutions and the sponsoring church concept for benevolence or missions.

---

[28] 21st Century Christian Publishing; P.O. Box 40526; Nashville, TN 37204-0526.

ME - Mutual Edification: NI and generally oppose using one preacher to present most of the sermons, but do have separate Bible classes.

NC - Non-class: NI and oppose having separate Bible classes as well as a located preacher.

NCp - Non-class (NC), but either uses or does not oppose the use of a located preacher.

OC - One Cup: NI, one container use in communion, no separate Bible classes.

OC+c - One Cup (OC) congregation, but separate Bible classes are allowed.

OCa - One Cup (OC) congregation using unfermented fruit of the vine and one loaf which is divided only as the participant takes his/her own portion.

OCb - OC, using unfermented fruit of the vine and one loaf, but the loaf is broken before distribution.

OCc - OC, using fermented fruit of the vine.

It is imperative for the remainder of this entire study, that the reader please take the time to realize, understand, and to always remember, that all nine of the above-noted little sub-divisions of the larger, overall division known as 'non-institutionalism' (or 'anti-ism'), are listed, recognized, and categorized together under that one heading for one very obvious reason: **They all come about as the result of a very similar mindset and reasoning process.** And that is a mindset and reasoning process which brother Rusty Stark so simply, eloquently, and yet so very profoundly explored and explained in his article, "Just Who Or What Is An 'Anti?'"[29] That article is excerpted at length below. It provides the reader with a preliminary overview of a few of the reasonings which will be biblically examined at much greater length in later chapters (***Emphasis*** added - DED):

> "'Liberalism' is the effort to take the 'binding' things of the pattern and 'unbind' them – to take the things we must or must not do and put them into the category of options.

---

[29] *Seek The Old Paths*, Vol. 17, No. 7; July 2006.

Anti-ism, on the other hand, is the effort to **bind things God has not bound**, to take the **options** in God's pattern (which is the New Testament) and put them into the category of **obligation**. Liberalism seeks to **loose the law God has bound**. Anti-ism seeks to **make laws that God has not bound**...

In 1 Timothy 4, Paul deals with false teachers. In verse three he mentions two specific false doctrines that represent a departure from the faith: 1) *forbidding to marry,* and 2) *commanding to abstain from meats*. Marriage (so long as one is free to marry) and the eating of meats are **options** (1 Cor. 7:2; Rom. 14). To **forbid** these things is to be 'anti' or against the things **God has allowed**. In 1 Timothy 4:1, Paul [condemns] these attempts to **make laws God has not made** ...

In Matthew 15... The scribes and Pharisees wanted to condemn the disciples for not washing their hands before they ate. This was not a law of God, it was a law of men. **Men had no right to make such laws** and Jesus condemns them for teaching the commandments of men...

Following is a partial list of some things some brethren are 'against' because they try to turn **options** into **obligations**:

> **Anti Bible Classes** – This teaching declares that dividing into classes divides the assembly and is not authorized by God's word. This is ... setting up a law that small groups of Christians cannot come together and study the Bible (Bible study). Paul taught both publicly and house to house (Acts 20:20). We learn by example that brethren in the first century met together on the first day of the week to worship (Acts 20:7; 1 Cor. 14) and from that example we learn we must assemble together for worship also. However, in addition to worshiping together, it is also appropriate that we study the Bible in smaller groups (cf. 2 Tim. 2:15).

Who would declare that it is sinful for brethren to study the Bible together?

- **Anti multiple cups in the Lord's Supper** – This teaching **_demands_** that only one cup be used in partaking the Lord's Supper. (Interestingly enough, my father attended a congregation where they opposed multiple cups, but they actually had two cups, one for each side of the aisle.) This ... places emphasis on the word 'cup' (singular) and fails to recognize that it is actually the contents of the cup that is being referred to. Paul quotes Jesus as saying, *this cup is the New Testament in my blood* (1 Cor. 11:25) – an obvious reference to the contents rather than the cup. In the next verse, Paul refers to drinking the cup. This is a **_physical impossibility unless he is referring to the contents of the cup_**.

- **Anti Cooperation** – This doctrine teaches that a church cannot take money from its treasury and assist another congregation in doing the Lord's work... We find congregations cooperated with each other in the New Testament (Rom. 15:26). Paul (by inspiration) wrote to the church in Corinth (as he taught other churches) and instructed Christians to give a weekly contribution into a treasury (1 Cor. 16:1-2). A good portion of this money (if not all of it) was taken to the elders of the church in Jerusalem for distribution (Acts 11:30; see also 2 Cor. 9:12-13). Furthermore, when Paul left Philippi, he travelled to Athens and then to Corinth (Acts 16-18). He later wrote the Philippians that no other church had supported him (communicated – giving and receiving) except the congregation in Philippi (Phil. 4:15). However, he wrote to the Corinthians that while he was with them, he robbed other churches (plural) in taking wages from them but not from Corinth (2 Cor. 11:8). If no one but

Philippi communicated with him in giving and receiving, but he was getting wages from other churches, Philippi must have been receiving contributions from other congregations and forwarding them to Paul. This is a clear example of church cooperation.

- **Anti Children's homes.** The argument is made that the responsibility to care for orphans (James 1:27) is the individual responsibility of each Christian, and therefore the church cannot be charged with such care. This is clearly wrong, for the same verse enjoins taking care of widows, and the church can be charged for widows (if they are widows indeed – 1 Tim. 5:9-16). If the church can be charged for the care of widows, then it can be charged for the care of needy children.

- **Anti aid to non-Christians.** This doctrine says that the contributions made in the New Testament were for the saints (Christians) only. They conclude from this that it is wrong to take money from the church treasury to help those who are not Christians. But, Galatians 6:10 says, '*As we have therefore opportunity, let us do good unto* ***all men****, especially unto them who are of the household of faith.*' They argue that Galatians 6:10 commands individuals, not churches, to help all men, and that the contribution is for the saints. This too can easily be proven false. For one, the instructions given in Galatians was for the 'churches of Galatia' (Gal. 1:2). And two, the contribution commanded in 1 Corinthians 16:1-2 was used for Christians and non-Christians. Paul says in 2 Corinthians 9:12 that the contribution had supplied the *want of the saints* and in verse 13 refers to the *distribution unto them* (saints), and unto *all men* (non-saints)."

As one reads through and explores the above excerpts from brother Stark's brief synopsis of the several different but eerily similar reasonings regarding the ties that bind all of these non-institutional type sub-groups, divisions, and categories together, his original point can be seen shining through throughout: The inevitable result of the entire Non-Institutionalist reasoning process, is to bind biblically-non-existent rules on men which God has definitely not bound, and to turn the options and freedoms in God's pattern into absolute obligations – or else. As brother Robby Eversole similarly echoed and alluded to during one of his *2015 Polishing The Pulpit* sessions: "Anti's take one way you can do something, and make it the ONLY way it can be done – or else…" (Please see *Appendix Study* in the back of this book for further exploration and clarification.)

Now, before going any further, please allow me to try to make my personal perspective of our 'one-cup' brethren just as crystal clear as I possibly can. I do not believe for one micro or millisecond that they are, or ever were, out to divide or destroy the Lord's church any more than any of the rest of us. I must say that I respect and admire completely what I believe to have been the original and ultimate motivation behind their perspective. I have to and do believe, that just like all their brethren who have also studied the Scriptures tirelessly, relentlessly, sincerely, and in an all-out effort and attempt to simply seek to please God and obey His will on other issues (or even who land on the other side of this one), that their intention and motivation was originally and only, to just purely and simply, please and obey God almighty to the very best of their ability and understanding.

I have to and do believe that their original intention and motivation was to not allow liberalism (the far left and total reverse of their mindset; the loosing of what God has absolutely bound) or any other false or cultural concept or doctrine to creep in and corrupt or pervert the absolute purity and simplicity of the God-breathed Scriptures for even one moment, or under any circumstances, just like the apostle Paul did (Galatians 2:5). In that respect we are no different; for I, too, am an "old paths" advocate (Jeremiah 6:16), seeking to be Berean in spirit (Acts 17:11; see also 2 Timothy 2:15);

sincerely and studiously trying with all my heart, soul, mind, strength and understanding, to be the kind of worshipper that God the Father is still seeking today (John 4:23-24).

However, if we truly study and trace down the origin and formation of the Pharisees during the intertestamental period, we will more than likely discover (depending on the particular resource that we choose to utilize on the subject) that they too, were apparently, originally the product of this same sort of dynamic. During a period of time when the religion of the Jews was reportedly being racked, rocked, inundated, and polluted with the temptation towards wholesale, Hellenistic, cultural and contemporary compromise, it was the newly-forming-out-of-necessity sect of the Pharisees that so stringently sought to stand against all such atrocities and impurities.

And yet, by the time of Jesus, the Pharisees were probably the group He admonished, rebuked, and reprimanded the most severely (See: Matthew 5:20, 22:34-23:39, and Luke 18:9-14 for example). Why? Was it because they insisted on keeping God's law to the letter just like when they began? No. Not on your eternal life. After all, Jesus Himself lived to do God's will (John 5:30, 6:38).

So, why His big problem with a group that had actually begun – from everything I understand – by being borne out of nothing but a distinct desire to ensure that God's perfect law was preserved, protected, and obeyed without compromise? Here's why: Because in their utter zeal to assure absolute and complete compliance with what they believed with all their heart that God wanted, they had sinfully gone way above and beyond what was actually written (1 Corinthians 4:6). They had thus circumvented and made "the word of God of no effect through [their] tradition which [they had] handed down" (Mark 7:13).

This they had done by inventing, incorporating, and insisting upon sub-rule after sub-sub-rule after sub-sub-sub rule regarding God's commandments. They had so micro-managed, redefined, and redirected everything God had commanded so far down as to completely nullify, neutralize, and/or circumvent anything God had originally said, meant, or intended. They were seeking to bind on men that which God had not bound, and in the process, were, according to Christ, straining out gnats while swallowing camels (See: Matthew 23:4, 13-24).

That is why Jesus had such a huge problem with, and so strongly condemned them and their doctrines, no matter how innocent, well-intended, or well-intentioned they might possibly have been at the outset (See: Matthew 5:20, 15:1-14; Mark 7:1-13).

This is apparently also the appropriate place to mention the 'principle of overcorrection' or 'over-emphasis.' When you drive a tractor-trailer up and down the northern portion of the eastern seaboard for a living for over 20 years, you learn a thing or two about overcorrecting – especially in a snowstorm. For example, when it comes to skidding or sliding on snowy and ice-covered roadways, if you start to skid or slide towards the left side of the road or ditch - or even wrongly believe or are somehow deceived into thinking that you might possibly be going into a skid or slide during a moment of misconception, misdirection, darkness, or misinformation - and you suddenly panic and therefore inadvertently overcorrect your steering, then, when it catches it can easily throw you into a hard and uncorrectable slide to the right, propelling you into the ditch on the other side of the road instead. Either way, either ditch, too far to the left or to the right and you don't make it to your desired destination. This, no matter how well-intentioned your attempts at course correction might have been or seemed to you at the time.

This 'principle of overcorrection' or over-emphasis also applies in the spiritual realm as well. Just because the medieval Catholic Church was not conducting baptism biblically did not give Martin Luther the authority to overcorrect and cast out baptism altogether in order to form his own, man-made and Biblically-defiant doctrine of salvation by 'faith only,' and therefore without baptism altogether (See: James 2:19-24). By so doing, although one would have to believe that it was surely not his original intention, he still fell into egregious error (only in a different direction) when it came to God's original New Testament doctrine regarding the essentiality of baptism both before and without which, salvation does not occur (John 3:3-5; Acts 2:37-47, 22:16; Romans 6:1-4; Galatians 3:26-27; Ephesians 4:4-6; Colossians 2:12; 1 Peter 3:21).

Perhaps the only scenario worse than that when it comes to this whole steering overcorrection illustration, would be if the loss of contact with the road surface and subsequent start of a slide towards the left were, in fact, not factual at all. In other words, if the driver of the rig only thought or perceived that he was starting to get off track to the left and therefore sought to jerk the wheel hard to the right in order to correct what he truly believed to be its erroneous course. What would happen then? Easy; the rig, which was originally and in reality in no danger whatsoever, would be totally wrecked as a direct result of nothing more than complete driver error, as he needlessly drove it off into the ditch on the right, due only and exclusively to his own misconception and resulting misplaced emphasis on, and attempt at, an otherwise completely needless course correction.

Now, while it is an inarguable fact that the church of our Lord has, in some locations, completely lost contact with the straight and narrow and strayed disastrously far to the left, all of the different and varying little bands, brands, divisions, and categories of the Non-Institutional sect and mindset of our beloved brotherhood can be condensed down into this one, major misconception: **Their perception that the church at large has lost contact with the scriptural straight and narrow and has gone into a hard slide to the left in several areas - which we can easily, biblically, and conclusively prove that it absolutely hasn't.** And so, in their well-intentioned but still misinformed attempts to correct a problem or problems that do not actually exist (except in their own perception), they insist on seeking to bind a totally needless hard right turn on every congregation of the Lord's church, which only proves disastrously divisive and detrimental to her overall mission to display a spirit of unity, and to ultimately deliver all of her once-lost souls, safely home to their heavenly destination.

It appears as if the Pharisees of Jesus' day had travelled down a similarly slippery spiritual slope. In their all-out attempts and efforts to avoid being overcome by spiritual error (both real as well as perhaps more imagined than in existence in some cases) to the one, left, or liberal side, they had completely overcorrected and gone so far in the opposite direction as to wind up spiritually wrecked, stranded, and stopped well short of their intended heavenly destination over in the other, or right hand ditch instead. In their relentless attempts to correct and stamp out any and all religious error whether real or perceived, they had, in reality, created and promoted far more religious error and division, but just simply of a different sort and in a different direction - and were still subsequently stuck and stopped short.

And although I completely believe that many of the leaders and promoters of some of these so-called "Non-Institutional" type doctrines never, ever, ever intended to cause any such needless, arbitrary, or unnecessary divisions and fractures within the Lord's one New Testament body or church, that is still the end result[30] of seeking to insist on a course correction for an error which, in reality, doesn't exist except within their own confused conclusions, by their relentlessly seeking to bind that which God never bound.

Speaking of which, do you recall Jesus' relating the account of what we refer to as 'The Good Samaritan' (Luke 10:30-37)? How important was that poor, pitifully-wounded, and beaten-up human being's body to Him? What about the affliction and suffering in the bodies of such poor beggars as blind Bartimaeus (Mark 10:46-52), the ten lepers (Luke 17:11-14), and so many others (Matthew 9:35-36, 15:29-30)? Additionally, what about Christ's appraisal of the reprisal He would render upon His return to those who had been entrusted with the health and care of His vineyard during His absence, but who refused to properly treat, respect, and love and care for it until His return (Matthew 21:33-46)? And then, consider this... If Jesus was that concerned over broken human bodies; and if He was that ready to mete out that level of retribution and destruction to those who did not properly and respectfully care for just His **vineyard** in their generation, what do you think He is going to do to any of those who might needlessly and superficially insist on cutting, dividing, severing, and fracturing His beloved and blood-bought body, bride, and church? Those to whom her care, health, and unity has been entrusted in this, our generation?

What would you do if it were you? What would you do if it were you and you had to leave your precious, priceless, and

---

[30] "No Such Thing As Individual Communion," The Christian Chronicle, last modified June 22, 2016, https://christianchronicle.org/no-such-thing-as-individual-communion/.

beloved bride in the care of another while you went away to take care of something vital; and then, upon your return for her, you found out that those whom you had entrusted with her care, had arbitrarily and needlessly cut, divided, wounded, and fractured her body – all without any truly viable or justifiable cause? What would you do? What do you think He's going to do? (Passages such as Hebrews 10:26-31 might provide just a terrifying sliver of a glimpse of insight into such…)

Look; certainly we all understand that there are some real, legitimate, God-commanded and Biblically-bound situations wherein there must be divisions in the beloved body, bride, or church of Christ over doctrine (Romans 16:16-18; 1 Corinthians 5:1-13, 11:19). But at the same time, surely we all must also understand and accept the biblical truth that any needless division involving prior misperceptions, personal misunderstandings, and/or pridefully-promoted agendas are just as wrong (1 Corinthians 1:10, 4:6; Galatians 5:19-20).

Sadly, as we shall surely see upon deeper scriptural investigation, the spirit of the Pharisees and the principle of overcorrection and over-emphasis are still apparently alive and well in and amongst some local pockets of the Lord's people to this day. Hence, the primary purpose of this writing effort is not only to scripturally explore, assess, and help to understand the problem, but to hopefully help to begin healing this gaping, ghastly, and grisly wound in the beloved and embattled body and bride of Christ, regarding the 'one-cup' sect, section, or division thereof today.

"The Pharisees were offended when they heard this saying" (Matthew 15:12). I'm sure they were. Those religious leaders who would stop at nothing to bind where God had not bound in the first century were deeply offended at Jesus as He relentlessly preached and proclaimed the unadulterated word of God to them, just as I'm sure that there may be some today who might be offended when they hear or read what is written herein from the word of God as well.

However, for those who would truly pause to thoroughly consider these chapters in light of the Scriptures, can you even begin to imagine the invincible force for Christ that we could truly become in our lost world today, were we all but to completely humble ourselves before God, get on the same spiritual page, teach the same divinely-inspired doctrine, and become the one, same, united and unified church and answer to Jesus' prayer which He prayed we'd be the very night before He was crucified (John 17:20-23; 1 Corinthians 4:17, 7:17, 11:16, 16:1-2)?

Wouldn't it be wonderful to help steer toward the day when a new *Churches of Christ in the United States* directory could be published, 'wherein there was neither one cup nor non-institutional, no no-class nor instrumental, nor male or female pride and power driven agendas, but that we were all truly one in Christ Jesus...' instead of a house divided and therefore in danger of falling, according to none other than the Lord Jesus Christ Himself (Matthew 12:25)?

NOTES

Chapter Four:

The Conceptualization

Before proceeding on into the primary portion of this book wherein the actual, contextual, 'rubber meets the road' biblical exploration of the 'one cup' doctrine begins in earnest, there are several things which the reader needs to be made acutely aware of. These include elements regarding everything from this effort's prior history, to the subsequent and ensuing results of this good sister's phone call, to some of the endearing encouragements and the series of events which eventually led to this book's publication. Other elements that many readers might not necessarily be aware of as of yet could include the vastly underestimated numbers and influence of the overall Non-Institutional movement's congregations, advancements, and adherents all around us today.

It was approximately a decade or so before this good sister ever called me that I first came into close contact with a member of the Non-Institutional sect or division of our beloved brotherhood, being duly introduced to the intricacies of some of their doctrines at that time. As I recall, it was only a few years into my very first full-time pulpit preaching position that a brother and preacher of that particular perspective who had lost his tiny, single-digit-in-attendance group of congregants about an hour and a half or so south of us contacted me. Seeing as how he actually only lived within a half-hour or so of where the congregation I worked with met for worship and study, he called to inquire as to whether or not it might be okay if he came and worshipped with us. Of course, I said yes.

As his story slowly unfolded, I quickly discovered that this man was certainly no slouch when it came to his integrity, intelligence, or involvement in the educational and evangelistic efforts of the Lord's church. He was fluent – dare I say, perhaps even expert – in several different languages. He had consistently conducted weekly Bible studies during his tour/tours of duty during the Gulf War. He had even biblically baptized some of the folks he had studied with into Christ for the forgiveness of their sins[31] in the pool waters of a particular foreign embassy – all the while with armed guards standing nearby and closely monitoring his every move!

Although I knew he appeared to have a bit of a different opinion or perspective regarding some spiritual things than what I was used to, I actually had no idea at the beginning, of either the origin of, the reasoning behind, or just how aggressively-held some of those viewpoints were. He had been baptized – born again of the water and the Spirit - in accordance with Scripture in order to be saved, and had subsequently been added by God to His Son's one, New Testament church, in complete compliance and obedient accordance with God's commandments in exactly the same manner as all of us had been (John 3:3-5; Acts 2:37-47, 22:16; Romans 6:1-4; Galatians 3:26-27; Ephesians 4:4-6; Colossians 2:12; 1 Peter 3:21). And from everything I saw and heard from him, he certainly seemed to totally accept, to completely believe in, and to steadfastly defend the eternal and inerrant, divinely-inspired and God-breathed nature of every word of Scripture (Psalm 19:7-11; 119; 2 Timothy 3:14-4:4; 2 Peter 1:16-21).

He was pumped, primed, and readily expecting to just 'jump right in' and start serving and teaching pretty much as soon as he showed up on the scene. Although I was somewhat green, inexperienced, uninformed and uneducated, not only as a fairly new full-time pulpit preacher, but particularly when it came to his obviously differing and varied doctrines and positions in some areas, I was still very wary. Sure, it would be absolutely wonderful to have another strong, willing, well-informed and well-educated, highly-experienced and biblically-knowledgeable co-worker to help and work alongside of in that corner of the kingdom. But, I strongly cautioned him to wait a while; to give the congregation time to get to know him; and to make sure we were all on the same page doctrinally before he began to get too heavily involved. This, so as not to split,

---

[31] Acts 2:38.

splinter, or confuse the congregation. He didn't listen, but sought to plunge right in anyway.

It didn't take too awfully long before some of his Non-Institutional doctrines came catapulting forth like a runaway locomotive. This forced an emergency Sunday afternoon men's business meeting wherein it was readily determined by those present that he would be immediately removed from all teaching, preaching, and serving roles, until and unless these differences were resolved via an in-depth Bible study with him. It was at that point that I had to really dive in and begin to educate myself quickly on this personally newly-discovered, doctrinal division within the Lord's church.

This brother had studied, preached, defended, and presented his particular perspective for a number of years, to a number of people, in a number of different countries all over the world. Shortly after his removal from all congregational service roles, he compiled and presented an in-depth list of scriptural references and reasonings (several of which came from Non-Institutional websites and internet resources as I recall) as to why his viewpoint was the only biblically-correct and acceptable one. During the course of the next several months' worth of back and forth, black and white, exhaustive and in-depth biblical study and examination, he finally came to the conclusion that what he had taught and defended over all those years was not only incorrect but was biblically indefensible when explored in the full and glaring light of biblical dissection and investigation. He thus repented, was restored, and began serving again.

Over the course of time (until my eventual departure from that congregation), there was more than once wherein he approached either myself or one of the other men of the church to thank us yet again for being willing to study the Scriptures with him and to subsequently help him see the errors of his previously-held perspective. It is my ardent hope and prayer that the same sort of unity and walking worthy of the Lord[32] might come about – only on a much larger and more widespread scale – as a result of this book's publication.

---

[32] Ephesians 4:1-3; Philippians 1:27.

Fast forward to a decade or so later and what happened in the aftermath of this good sister's previously-discussed communication with me. Not too long after her call, I had the privilege of having posted on brother Travis Main's outstanding *Church of Christ Articles* website (www.churchofchristarticles.com), a trio of articles devoted solely to her call and the main topic thereof. It is from those articles that some of the material in this book comes. In fact, although this same concept will be more deeply and biblically explored later, it is from the first of those articles, "One Cup Call," that the following (slightly adapted) assessment comes:

> "But one of the saddest things associated with phone calls like that for me, lies in regards to what I consider to be one of the very simplest, most elementary, and most transparent and easy to see problems with the entire 'one cup' perspective. This sister's home congregation over closer to the east coast used one cup… while the Arkansas congregation with whom she and her family had worshipped previously – being one that also defends the 'one cup' doctrine as well - obviously used a different and additional cup from the one used at her home congregation… as do all four of the congregations I supplied her with contact information for will use yet more and different, separate cups from either her home congregation, the one in Arkansas, or one another… just as will every other 'one cup' congregation in the world. Does anyone else besides me see the incredible irony and complete contradiction here?
>
> The adherents and defenders of the 'one cup' doctrine claim to be disciples and members of Jesus' one, biblical, faithful New Testament church worldwide. They claim to believe in and defend a doctrine of Jesus' disciples all drinking from the same one cup during communion… And yet, at the very same time that they defend a doctrine that ultimately divides the body of Christ

by dividing them from those who claim that Jesus' disciples can actually take communion from different cups, they themselves actually also use different and multiple communion cups from one another when they are in different congregations and locations. They have to. It is a physical impossibility for all of Jesus' disciples today all over the world to literally use 'one cup.' It simply cannot be done.

Thus, while they defend their 'one cup' doctrine to the point of actually dividing the body of Christ over it, severing and seeing themselves differently from those of their brethren who don't insist on their particular 'one cup' perspective, they themselves actually use more than one cup every Sunday (from hundreds of other 'one cup' disciples congregating in other locations).

So which way is it? One cup, or multiple cups? One cup – absolutely no exceptions - as they insist upon during their doctrinal dissertations? Or one cup only when it is a matter of convenience - as they actually practice in reality? And how can any Christian condemn the use of more than one communion cup amongst their brethren, when each and every single one of the 'one cup' congregations they are a part of, uses a different cup from each and every other one of the 'one cup' congregations, each and every single Lord's Day? In other words, when they themselves, while defending 'one cup,' actually use multiple cups?

Which do **_you_** think is more important to the Lord: Preserving the unity of His one church which Jesus prayed and died and shed His blood for? Or, dividing that one church down over an absolute (and scripturally indefensible) insistence on only one communion cup and making it a test of faith and fellowship, while at the same time, actually using different - and therefore multiple – communion cups themselves from location to location? How is such a circumstance any different from what the apostle Paul condemned some of his first-century brethren in the congregation at Rome over in Romans 2:17-24?

And all the while, lost people drive by all our assemblies, headed for hell for all eternity, while some insist on sitting back and seeking to strain out a gnat while swallowing a camel; going beyond what is written through a total misunderstanding of illustrative, metaphorical language and usage; and insisting that those who don't share their misunderstanding thereof are hell-bound because of it. How sad. Yes; and how much more than sad do you think this is to the Savior who shed His blood for all of us?

If you are a member or a congregation of the one body of Christ that wants to continue to hold to the 'one cup' practice and perspective in the place where you worship, that is your business – we are all autonomous congregations. I certainly have no problem with how you, as my beloved brethren, conduct your communion service in your particular congregation in that regard. But please don't go beyond what is written by insisting that those who drink from multiple communion cups – just as you yourselves also do every Sunday from location to location – are somehow sinning by so doing, but that you somehow aren't.

We are all supposed to be one in Christ Jesus. When are we all going to start acting, loving, accepting, worshipping, serving, and fellowshipping like it? Because the day we do, maybe we can finally convince the world that the Christ is indeed real, and then just maybe we can start to make the difference Jesus always so desperately desired that His disciples would make (***John 17:20-23; Philippians 1:27***).

Also, within the past few years (February and March of 2014 to be exact), I had the express privilege of preparing and presenting an eight-lesson sermon mini-series on the doctrine of Non-Institutionalism as a whole. And then, two and a half years after that (in late August and early September of 2016), I had the further privilege of preparing and presenting an additional three-lesson sermon mini-series which was more specifically and exclusively devoted to just the topic of the 'one cup' doctrine itself. (That audio sermon set included some of the most listened to lessons out of the several hundred I had posted on a previous church website) Because of the very similar mindsets which led to both the larger, more all-inclusive, Non-Institutional division or section of our beloved brotherhood, as well as its smaller, sub-divisional 'one-cup' contingent, all of these lessons were summarily grouped and can be subsequently accessed together in the Non-Institutionalism collection of sermons at: https://Godswordistruth.org/sermons/.

Now obviously, with such an array of these materials currently posted out there on the internet, it was both inevitable and unavoidable that responses would start coming in... some positive, some not so much. I eventually heard from a 'one-cup' brother from over nearer the west coast somewhere who requested to study the issue with me. We exchanged several e-mail studies and lessons over time. He couldn't ever seem to quite adequately answer some of the more important biblical questions I had concerning his insistence on his 'one cup' teaching. He offered to put me in contact with some of the 'one-cup' brethren in nearby Tulsa to study with. He also strongly questioned why the good sister I referenced had ever called me in the first place. After all, he seemed insistent on the fact that such 'one-cup' congregations as she was looking for were not all that difficult to actually locate with but a little bit of research. And in this he was correct. I myself am no techno-geek to be sure. But within five minutes or so with an internet search engine, I must admit that it is pretty easy to locate a website or two featuring 'one-communion container' insistent congregations, should some-one really want to find one.

Another response to these now-posted resources was an incredibly powerful and positive one from an absolutely wonderful, faithful, mature, and grateful sister in Christ in central Ohio who contacted me to inform me of the epidemic growth in the number of Non-Institutional congregations and adherents in and around the area where she lived, and to constantly encourage me to write and get published what she considered to be such an essential and much-needed work in today's church of Christ climate.

And thirdly, finally, and most recently, I was once again completely surprised, humbled, and encouraged, to hear from a previously unknown-to-me brother and faithful fellow gospel preacher from the Nashville area who had, himself, grown up in the midst of a close-knit, so-called 'mainstream' group of congregations, but also in somewhat close proximity to a group of so-called "non-cooperative," "Non-Institutional," or "anti" brethren. After his recently having been requested by a 'one-cup' brother from Texas to have a long-distance Bible study with him on the issue, he, too, ran across some of the afore-mentioned materials, made contact with me, and in the course of our conversation, voiced how this contingent was making a resurgence in his area as well.

I don't tell you all of this to boast or brag or anything of the sort (Galatians 6:14). My reasons for telling you all of the above are primarily two-fold. First off, I want for you to know that what you are studying, discovering, and maybe even rediscovering from within these pages - and infinitely far more importantly of course, from within the sacred pages of God's holy word as referenced herein - is not the result of some spur of the moment, hastily-arrived at, emotionally-charged, and/or subjectively-driven series of convictions or conclusions. Quite to the contrary, they are the result of a sincere and over-the-years-long accumulation of serious and contextual biblical study, exploration, and common-sense application.

And secondly, I have also come to believe that the vast majority of 'everyday Christians in the pews' are pretty much oblivious to just how strong and widespread this particular sect, segment, division, and contingent of our beloved brotherhood currently is. When I first had the privilege of preaching the aforementioned, eight lesson, Non-Institutional sermon mini-series back in 2014, there was at least one decades-long member of the congregation here who had never heard of it. This, while the Non-Institutional doctrines are far closer, far more prominent, and far more powerfully and persuasively presented than most of us would probably ever imagine.

For example, while perusing and researching resources for that original series of sermons, I ran across one website that claimed there were 42 Non-Institutional congregations of the churches of Christ in Oklahoma alone. These included congregations in Catoosa, Claremore, Shidler, and Stillwater; in addition to the Southside congregation in Muskogee; the Stone Canyon congregation in Owasso; and the Woodland Hills congregation in Tulsa; as well as several prominent others. It has been reported that "This fellowship of Non-Institutional congregations… is estimated at about 120,000 members, accounting for around 9% of the members of Churches of Christ in the United States, and for about 15% of congregations."[33]

Further research has since revealed, that when it comes to the 'one cup' sub-division, of the larger, Non-Institutional division of our beloved brotherhood, that, "In 2009, there were 551 'One Cup' churches with 17,313 members, mostly located in Texas. Almost all these churches were congregations without Sunday Bible Schools."[34]

Additionally, according to the June 22, 2016 issue of *The Christian Chronicle*, in an interview with one of their leading and more well-known advocates it was similarly reported that, "The most recent volume of the directory *Churches of Christ in the United States*, published by *21st Century Christian*, lists 553 one-cup congregations with a combined membership of 18,929. Most do not have separate Bible classes and partake the Lord's Supper from an undivided loaf of unleavened bread and one cup."[35]

---

[33] "The churches of Christ (non-institutional)," Wikipedia, accessed June 21, 2018, https://en.wikipedia.org/wiki/The_churches_of_Christ_(non-institutional).

[34] "My Conversation With A One Cup Church," West University church of Christ, Roy Rodes, September 17, 2015, http://www.westuchurch.com/2015/09/17/my-conversation-with-a-one-cup-church.

[35] "No Such Thing As Individual Communion," Christian Chronicle, Lynn McMillon, June 22, 2016, http://www.christianchronicle.org/article/no-such-thing-as-individual-communion.

Speaking of yet further widespread but still possibly underestimated influence, that same, June 2016, *Christian Chronicle* article went on to reveal the fact that their television show, *Let the Bible Speak*, "a TV program produced for more than 40 years by Ronny Wade" and now "on Springfield's NBC affiliate... airs on 32 other stations that reach 21 states and Canada. In addition, Kevin Presley hosts '*Let the Bible Speak*' in Fort Smith, [Arkansas], and Monroe, [Louisiana]. Brandon Stephens and Shahe' Gergian host the program in Columbia, [Missouri]." Yes, their doctrinal insistence on one communion cup has a very wide-spread area and avenue of influence, and a good-sized and very convicted number of adherents.

In conclusion, I have several hopes for when all is said, done, and studied with the information assembled in this book. I hope and pray that the Lord God almighty might somehow use its scriptural message and common-sense contents to bring about some much-needed measure of understanding, repentance, healing, humbling, unity, and healthy growth once again within His one, blood-bought bride's currently wounded and divided body; within the precious and priceless body or church which He has entrusted to our care in this generation.

As one of our Non-Institutional brethren from Missouri actually wrote to me several years ago in an e-mail regarding certain elements of this same topic (along with its attached 70-page booklet defining and defending their doctrine): "*I pray you all will receive this with the love in which it is sent. Always remember: 'When a man/woman who is honestly mistaken hears the truth, he/she will either quit being mistaken, or cease to be honest.*'" I can only hope that that good brother as well as many others just like him might somehow be exposed to this material; that they might seriously, honestly, humbly, and objectively reconsider and re-study their own previously-held and preached convictions as I have had to; and that they then will take to heart his very own words of wisdom once sent to me as italicized above.

And I also hope that maybe, just maybe, that somehow that good and anonymous sister whom I've never met or heard from again, but whose one phone call that particular spring day has been used by God to set in motion an incredible chain of events which eventually culminated in this book's publishing, might find a copy of it; share and study its biblical contents with her husband, family, and home congregation; and then someday, that just maybe she and her family might find their way to worship with the congregation here. God bless.

NOTES

Chapter Five:

The Confusion (Part One)

The Scripture very clearly, concisely, and emphatically states in 1 Corinthians 14:33, that: "God is not the author of confusion, but of peace…" If one were to read the entire fourteenth chapter of 1 Corinthians for context sake, they would readily see that the first-century worship assembly of the Lord's church in Corinth was in utter chaos, confusion, and meltdown mode. It appears to have more resembled the ungodly mob assembled to reject and rebel against God as reported in Acts 19:23-34, than it did what the Lord's church assembled in humble adoration and to offer worship in spirit and truth to almighty God should have looked like. Prophets, teachers, tongue-speakers, revelation-receivers, interpreters, and women of acute curiosity were apparently loudly competing for attention and answers as they all sought to shout and cry out at the same time. Therefore, their 'worship' assembly confusion more closely resembled a mob-like mass hysteria than the reverent worship of the God of peace and order which they professed.

Now, while that might not seem to have much to do with our current 'one cup' doctrinal discussion, it has everything to do with it, primarily because of one, glaring, colossal, essential, elemental, and golden nugget of truth which that text contains, and which we must not, and cannot, afford to miss. That essential truth is the one which is found in verse thirty-three: "God is not the author of confusion, but of peace…" This crucial and critical 'balm of Gilead' truth is absolutely imperative to our continued study, and its proper biblical conclusion, application, and hopefully subsequent healing of the beleaguered body of Christ.

The actual "author" (or originator) of confusion is surely none other than Satan himself. It was he who first muddied the waters and caused the confusion of God's clear-cut, extremely simple and easy to understand commandment not to eat of the tree of the knowledge of good and evil in the Garden of Eden (Genesis 2:16-17). Satan easily caused this confusion in Eve's mind simply by tying a satanic "not" into the flawless fabric of God's commandment (Genesis 3:1-4). He did that in exactly the same fashion and manner as he continually seeks to tie a satanic "not" into the very divinely-designed and flawless fabric of every other one of God's all-authoritative commandments. This includes God's commandment which we find in the same text from whence our current truth under consideration comes. Satan repeatedly does the same thing which he did in the Garden of Eden to Eve, whenever he gets any of her daughters to believe, accept, and militantly advocate that 'women [*NOT*] keep silent in the churches' (See 1 Corinthians 14:34).

Furthermore, it is quite easily provable that Satan is the original author, perpetrator, and promoter of all such biblically-contradicting and counteracting confusion. Whether we are discussing the confusion those sought to cause who were seeking to thwart the ongoing progress of God's faithful and hard-working people in places like Nehemiah 4:1-8, Acts 19:23-32, or others, James 3:13-18 could not be any clearer about where all such confusion of biblical commandments and communication comes from:

> "Who *is* wise and understanding among you? Let him show by good conduct *that* his works *are done* in the meekness of wisdom. But if you have bitter envy and self-seeking in your hearts, do not boast and lie against the truth. This wisdom does not descend from above, but *is* earthly, sensual, demonic. For where envy and self-seeking *exist,* confusion and every evil thing *are* there. But the wisdom that is from above is first pure, then peaceable, gentle, willing to yield, full of mercy and good fruits, without partiality and without hypocrisy. Now the fruit of righteousness is sown in peace by those who make peace."

Now, while we understand that "God is not the author of confusion, but of peace," we also understand that He has, on occasion, utilized the tool of confusion in order to accomplish His divine purposes, on both His enemies, as well as those of His own people who would choose to try to subvert and circumvent His will in the past (Genesis 11:1-9; Exodus 23:27; Deuteronomy 28:15-28; 1 Samuel 7:10; Psalm 60:1-3; Isaiah 45:16). But if and when people do not want to truly seek, sincerely study, honestly understand, and humbly accept and obey God's divine truth, order, commandments, and revelation as written (2 Thessalonians 2:9-15), then... what other result should they realistically expect, except confusion?

Although Satan is evil incarnate, he is certainly not stupid, nor is he unobservant. After Jesus used Scripture to thwart Satan in the first temptation he perpetrated on the Christ in the wilderness (as recorded in Matthew 4:1-4), it would seem that Satan, when he saw how successful Jesus had been by utilizing Scripture in order to defeat him there, then sought to turn the tables and use Scripture on Jesus (Matthew 4:5-6).

In similar fashion, it would appear at least to this writer, that Satan must surely have also seen and heard how wonderfully successful God was at accomplishing His ends when He confused the people's language in Genesis 11:1-9. God stated therein that, "Behold, they are one people, and they have all one language, and this is only the beginning of what they will do. And nothing that they propose to do will now be impossible for them. Come, let us go down and there confuse their language, so that they may not understand one another's speech" (Verses 6-7 ESV).

Many, varied, and widespread today are the examples that could be cited of where Satan has so incredibly and successfully divided people, simply by confusing their understanding of that communication which would otherwise make them one and ultimately allow them to accomplish anything for God. Just a few of the soul-damning and endangering examples of where Satan has perpetrated such utter confusion as to cause the complete and subsequent breakdown of proper biblical communication and conclusions, can be found regarding such biblical words and phrases as "church," "works," "pastors," "baptism," "salvation," "faith only," "one body," and "prayer of faith." If you ask the leaders of almost any major denomination known to man today about the specific meanings and usages of these biblical words and phrases, and then compare the answers they give to what God said and defined them as in Scripture, you can verify almost without exception, just how completely successful Satan's campaign of corrupting and confusing God's biblical communication to man has been.

For clarity sake, let us briefly re-state and conclude before continuing: God is not the author of confusion, but of peace (1 Corinthians 14:33). God, Christ, and the Holy Spirit operate as One, in complete and perfect unity and harmony with one another (John 5:30, 6:38, 14:9-11, 16:12-15). In like manner, Their true disciples are to do the same (John 17:16-26, Ephesians 4:1-6), being of the same mind as Them and one another (Romans 12:14-16, 15:5-6; 1 Corinthians 1:10; 2 Corinthians 13:11; Philippians 1:27-2:8, 3:15-19; Hebrews 8:10; 1 Peter 3:8-12). God's commandments as to how to accomplish that complete and perfect harmony and unity are neither burdensome nor confusing (1 John 5:2-3; 1 Corinthians 14:33).

Therefore, wherever there is chaos, confusion, discord, disunity, and division, it is pretty much universally because Satan has come in and caused chaos and confusion in our minds, as to the truth of God's clear-cut communication and commandments (James 3:13-17). And considering our current contextual discussion of the 'one cup' doctrine, it seems that nowhere is this Satanically-engineered campaign of language confusion, corruption, and chaos much more obvious or devastating than when it comes to the divisions and denominations it has caused within the blood-bought borders of our own beloved brotherhood. Consider the following…

There are certain things which we all automatically do many times over the course of a normal day without so much as even a second thought, a second of conscious effort, or a second of hesitation. These would include things like blinking and breathing to name but a couple. When was the last time you had to consciously think, reason, process, convince, and/or push yourself to do either of those things every time you blinked or breathed in or out over the course of a whole day? Obviously, you didn't. You did them without thinking. You didn't have to. You do them so often and so automatically that they just come naturally or as "second-nature" to you.

The same is true in the way we speak, communicate, and understand others – including God and His word – as well. There are some very simple, little, basic literary tools which we so commonly use, utilize, encounter, and experience in our everyday lives, that processing and understanding them has become an almost inevitably automatic, subconscious, and unrealized process for most of us. These little literary tools of communication are what we would commonly refer to as "figures of speech." These include such categories as parables, illustrations, similes, and metaphors. They are not at all difficult to understand or comprehend, up until and unless of course we encounter them in the word of God. And then, in steps Satan, the author of confusion, and all of the sudden, some folks who use such figures of speech on a daily, hourly, or even minute by minute basis, don't seem to be able to understand the first thing about how to recognize, distinguish, understand, categorize, correctly apply, or implement them at all in many cases. This is precisely the situation that lies at the center of so much of the current confusion and division coming from within and amongst so many of our 'one-cup' congregations:

The confusion that comes about as a result of the complete failure to recognize and distinguish the difference between when Jesus is speaking in literal terms, and when He is using a figure of speech.

Let the reader completely understand, and concretely impress upon their internal, psychological, and spiritual hard drive, the contents of that one, far-reaching, and all-encompassing sentence. There is no more simple, fundamental, or foundational key to understanding, unlocking, and overcoming this whole, congregational division-causing 'one cup' ball of wax, than is contained right there in that one, simple, easy to understand sentence.

In fact, as absolute proof-positive that we commonly and continually utilize and process countless figures of speech on a regular and daily basis without even thinking about it or even momentarily considering taking them literally, did you catch the figures of speech I just purposely used as you read the previous sentence? I just did it twice; no, at least three times in fact, in just the previous few sentences! I purposefully used several, simple figures of speech – a common practice which we utilize and process on a regular basis without even thinking about it numerous times a day in our conversations.

For example, even though I used the term "key," you surely did not think I meant a literal, physical, metal, "can be held in your hand and used to literally unlock something tangible" *'key'* just then as I wrote of the "key to understanding," did you? And especially one that could be used to literally unlock a literal, physical, **"ball of wax**," which was also a simple figure of speech which you probably processed without even thinking about it as well, right? And certainly, you understood without consciously thinking about it, that you couldn't possibly, literally, **"catch"** something you read, unless someone threw what it was written on to you, didn't you?

What about those figures of speech which I also purposely placed in a few of the previous portions of this chapter? You read right through them, processed them, and understood they were not to be taken literally under any circumstances whatsoever didn't you? For example, when I used the figure of speech, **"muddied the waters"** in the second sentence of the third paragraph of this chapter in reference to what Satan has done to God's commandments, you didn't for a moment confuse that with the thought of his literally stirring up the bottom or adding more mud to an actual body of literal water did you? No. You knew better without thinking about it.

What about in the seventh paragraph of this chapter when I referred to Satan's seeking to **"turn the tables"** on Jesus by using Scripture on Him during Christ's second recorded temptation in the wilderness? Did you even pause momentarily, to possibly consider taking that phrase literally; that there was a real, literal table on a carousel out there? No; of course not. That would be both silly and ridiculous as well as causing completely unnecessary and unwarranted confusion. You just simply, automatically, and immediately understood without even so much as a second thought, that there was no literal table there that Satan actually picked up and spun around on top of Jesus, but that I was using a "figure of speech" which was not to be taken literally.

What about all of the figures of speech I also premeditatedly and purposefully placed into the fifth paragraph of Chapter Four? Did you take it literally when I referred to the previously Non-Institutional brother as being "pumped," "primed," and ready to just "jump right in?" I certainly hope not. In fact, I know you didn't. You couldn't have. This, because if you had, you would probably still be back there lost in hopeless confusion.

What about in the very next sentence when I remarked that I was "green?" Did you stop to wonder how I had actually and literally changed my skin color? Of course not. What about a few sentences later when I used the phrase about us all being "on the same page?" Did you really and truly think I meant that we were all actually, literally standing together on one, lone, huge, colossal, literal sheet of paper, somehow bound into some gigantic book? No.

Do you begin to see how easily, automatically, and subconsciously we all utilize and process countless figures of speech on a daily and often hourly basis? Amongst the hundreds of similar, everyday, never-to-be-taken-literally at all, common figures of speech which we might encounter over the course of a day or two, could easily include such phrases as:

- "Raining cats and dogs." –Have you ever seen that literally happen (or stepped in a 'poodle')?
- "Right out straight." –So, if the person who says that isn't lying down in an arrow straight position when they make that statement, do you really call them a liar?
- "In a pickle." –You'd have to either be really small or start with a really huge cucumber, wouldn't you?
- "Between a rock and a hard place." –We understand that this just means to be in a difficult position, or having to make a difficult choice, don't we?

- "Drew a blank." –Think about that... How can you literally draw something that isn't there?
- "Swamped with homework." So... if there's no swamp in your area to do homework in, does that mean you don't have to ever do any more homework?
- "Bombed the test." –Do you understand that to mean the person literally took a plane up and dropped a bomb on their exam?
- "A handful of people" –They either must have been very little people, or else the person speaking must have had very large hands if that's to be taken literally!
- "Broken-hearted." –If that were literal, then anyone in that condition would be dead... wouldn't they?
- "The sun set." –I didn't know it was standing up to begin with... Does the sun even have 'a leg to stand on?'
- "They coughed up the money." –So... you actually believe when you say or hear that, that the person literally swallowed the money to begin with?
- "On a roll." –Dinner, Kaiser, hot dog, or hamburger roll?
- "New cell phone with four lines." –News flash: Cell phones don't have 'lines' – literally! That's what makes them 'cell' phones!
- "Right lane must turn right." This was the wording on a roadside sign I recently saw. The fact is, that that lane never actually, literally went anywhere; it just laid right there. Although there was a literal "right lane" right there, the instructions did not refer to the literal lane itself turning right, but the term "right lane" was actually being used only as a figure of speech to refer to any vehicles that might ever travel on or over it.

In addition to those few listed above, there are countless other figures of speech we use, hear, and process without any conscious effort on an everyday basis, which, if taken literally, would only cause widespread confusion and ridiculous and unrealistic conclusions. (In fact, to continually emphasize this very vital 'point' about how constantly and continually we use and process such figures of speech without even thinking about it, you will find a few 'sprinkled in' and noted with single quotation marks throughout the remainder of this book.)

For example, we readily realize (thanks to figures of speech), that the person actually, literally, standing upright in front of, and conversing with us, can also, at the exact same time, be said to be '*falling* in love,' '*setting* the pace,' '*running* for office,' '*in* over their head,' '*up* to no good,' or any number of other figurative postures and positions. But what if somebody who refused to accept and acknowledge the difference between literal language and figures of speech for whatever reason, absolutely insisted on your accepting and acknowledging that the person who was actually, literally, and in reality standing still right there in front of you, was actually, literally, and in reality, *falling*, *setting*, or *running* at the same time? Chaos, confusion, and hopelessly divided and irreconcilable conclusions would be the only possible result, wouldn't they?

It should be incredibly clear at this point, that one of the most effective 'tools' (although it is not an actual, literal, physical, can-be-held-in-your-hand "tool") which Satan, the author of confusion 'employs' (although he cannot actually, literally, and in reality "hire out" any concept) to confuse and divide us regarding God's communication to us so that we can't spiritually be the "one body" (or church) which as God wants, is the failure in some 'corners' of both the religious world at large as well as within our own beloved brotherhood (even though they may not be actual, literal, 45 degree angle "corners" necessarily), to rightly 'divide the word' (and no, we're not actually going to be literally cutting it in two) and differentiate between when God is speaking in **literal**, as opposed to **illustrative**, **figurative**, **metaphoric**, **apocalyptic**, or **parabolic** language. Consider with me, the following examples of this…

Some religious groups today – whether intentionally or not - erroneously seek to superimpose and/or interject a literal definition both onto and into, all of the often symbolic and apocalyptic language of the Book of Revelation. This causes untold confusion and misconception regarding its beautiful and victorious message of hope and comfort from God for His beleaguered people. In fact, Satan has been so successful at causing this confusion of God's communication in this manner, that many religious people today won't even study its message, "Because it's too confusing."

Citing only one of countless examples from Revelation that could be given of this egregious and eternally-fatal error, some religious groups militantly insist that we must translate all of God's SYMBOLIC numbers in that book, absolutely LITERALLY, such as when it comes to things like the "thousand years" of Revelation 20:1-7. But the word "thousand" there is completely symbolic and not to be taken any more literally than when its Hebrew equivalent is translated in Psalm 50:10, wherein God says: "For every beast of the forest *is* Mine, *and* the cattle on a thousand hills." Now, if anyone were to insist on that word "thousand" as being absolutely literal and binding instead of being a figure of speech (in much the same manner as so many of our precious 'one cup' brethren so often do with the word "cup"), it would cause nothing but untold confusion, error, and even biblical contradiction. Think about it. If the word "thousand" there in that Psalm is to be taken literally, then, upon which hill does one start counting? One in Australia? One in England? How about a hill in Siberia, South America, or the United States? And if so, which one? And what happens when one gets to the one thousandth hill in their count? Do the cattle on the one thousandth and first hill belong to someone else? If so, to whom? And if they belonged to someone else other than God, then that would also contradict verse twelve, which says "…for the world *is* Mine, and **_all_** its fullness" (**_emphasis_** added - DED).

The essential lesson learned from just that one biblical example of figurative language and God's explanation and clarification of it within the next verse or two must be noted, emphasized, ingrained, and remembered throughout the remainder of our 'one cup' study. And that vital and essential lesson is simply this: In verse twelve, God clearly defines, explains, and emphasizes exactly what He meant by the figure of speech which He had just used in verse ten. In verse twelve, God makes it clear that what He meant when He spoke figuratively of "the cattle on a thousand hills" in verse ten, was that everything on earth belongs to Him. And as we shall see, this is exactly, precisely, and consistently what He does throughout the four gospel accounts whenever Jesus refers to a "cup" with reference to communion: He clarifies within the immediately-following few sentences, that what He meant when He spoke figuratively of the "cup," was the fruit of the vine it contained.

But for now, and in reference to Psalm 50:10-12, do you begin to see the absolute and unending mess, confusion, and religious error one can get hopelessly and inevitably 'mired' in, the moment they fail to understand and/or discern the difference between when God is using literal language, and when He is using a figure of speech?

However, this failure to rightly understand, divide, and/or discern the difference between when God is using literal language as opposed to when He is using figurative language, is not limited to just those seeking Him today. It was a problem in His day as well. If you read John 6:35-66, you will see that there was a group of Jesus' own disciples with Him as He taught in the synagogue at Capernaum who later walked away because of this ***very same failure*** to recognize the difference between when He was using figurative language, as opposed to using literal language! See for yourself by re-reading that text in your own Bible.

NOTES

Chapter Six:

The Confusion (Part Two)

In the previous chapter, we only began to 'scratch the surface' of some of the unending confusion and erroneous conclusions that can occur when any person or group of religious persons fail (whether through biblical ignorance or knowledgeable intention) to understand and/or discern the difference between when God and/or Jesus are using literal language, and when They are using figurative language, or, in other words, one of the different, specific figures of speech as defined below. (Please note: completely understanding this difference is absolutely essential to our understanding of the entire communion "cup" issue, and our subsequent healing of the division that the deadly lack of such discernment and understanding has caused among us in the body of Christ.) We now continue that discussion in this chapter.

Webster's New World College Dictionary; Fourth Edition[36] defines "figure of speech" as: "an expression, as a metaphor or simile, using words in a non-literal sense or unusual manner to add vividness, beauty, etc. to what is said or written."

Figures of speech come in a variety of forms. The following definitions of a few of the more commonly known figures of speech are taken from that same Webster's Dictionary:

- **Parable:** "An allegorical relation, ...an analogy, ...a short, simple story, usually of an occurrence of a familiar kind, from which a moral or religious lesson may be drawn."

---

[36] *Webster's New World College Dictionary; Fourth Edition* (New York: IDG Books Worldwide, Inc., 1999)

Perhaps one of the better examples of just such a parable (or parabolic language) from the entire Old Testament (although there are many) is the one found in the book of Ezekiel, Chapter 23 (which please take a moment to stop, read, and study right now). As the *New Unger's Bible Dictionary*[37] says regarding that chapter under the name "Oholah" ("a probably imaginary harlot, used by Ezekiel... as a symbol of the idolatry of Samaria"): "The allegory is an epitome of the history of the Jewish People."

The *New Unger's Bible Dictionary* goes on to further state, under the name "Oholibah," "A symbolical name given to Jerusalem, under the figure of an adulterous harlot."

The point is, that the first thirty-five verses of that chapter (at the least), are 'chocked full' of figures of speech, not to be taken literally. For example, one cannot literally 'cast God behind their back' (vs. 35). It is also extremely important to note that although the word "cup" is used a total of three times in two verses in that chapter (vss. 32-33), it is NOT talking about some lone, singular, literal, physical, can-be-held-in-your-hand cup whatsoever. After all, look at what that "cup" is full of in those verses. The word "cup" there in that particular parable is not to be taken as a literal cup but is simply used as a figure of speech.

New Testament biblical examples of the same type of figure of speech known as a parable are obviously in evidence throughout Matthew 13 and other texts. Jesus used them a lot: "...And without a parable He did not speak to them, that it might be fulfilled which was spoken by the

---

[37] New Unger's Bible Dictionary (Chicago: Moody Publishers, 1988)

prophet, saying: *'I will open My mouth in parables; I will utter things kept secret from the foundation of the world.'"* (Matthew 13:34-35).

- **Hyperbole:** "Exaggeration for effect and not meant to be taken literally (Ex.: He's as strong as an ox)."

Hyperbole then, is a type of figure of speech which purposefully exaggerates for the sake of emphasis. We see biblical examples of the Lord's usage of hyperbole in places like Matthew 18:8-9, Luke 14:26, and others. If one didn't understand that Jesus wasn't being utterly literal in those passages but was instead using a figure of speech, then they would probably wind up either mortally wounding, blinding, or injuring themselves or some of their family members in a totally misled but futile attempt to try to please and follow Jesus!

- **Simile:** "A figure of speech in which one thing is likened to another, dissimilar thing by the use of *like, as,* etc. (Ex.: a heart as big as a whale, her tears flowed like wine): distinguished from METAPHOR."

For a plethora of biblical examples of this particular type of figure of speech, please see the Song of Solomon, wherein in the New King James Version, the word "like" occurs some thirty-six times in eight short chapters, while the word "as" occurs another twenty-one times, for a grand combined total of some fifty-seven occurrences of these two terms of similitude in that short little book.

It is also noteworthy to mention here, that sometimes there is an overlapping of applicable terms when it comes to specific figures of speech. For instance, as all can surely see and understand from the above definition, Jesus' parables as recorded in Matthew 13 and other places were also, at the same time, similes: "The kingdom of heaven is *like*..."

- **Metaphor:** According to Webster, a compound word of Greek origin, formed from the combining of the Greek word "*meta*," meaning "over," and "*pherein*," meaning "to bear." Hence, literally: "to carry over." "A figure of speech containing an implied comparison, in which a word or phrase ordinarily and primarily used of one thing, is applied to another. (Ex.: 'the curtain of night,' 'all the world's a stage.')"

    The **Learner's definition of 'metaphor'** includes the following:

    1: a word or phrase for one thing that is used to refer to another thing in order to show or suggest that they are similar.

    2: an object, activity, or idea that is used as a symbol of something else...[38]

Daily examples of metaphorical language might include such phrases as: "He swallowed his pride," "They swallowed the story, hook, line, and sinker," or "You are the wind beneath my wings."

Our entire Bibles, as well as the specific teaching of the Lord Jesus Christ Himself, is absolutely 'running over' with just such metaphorical figures of speech. Metaphors seemed to be one of our Lord's favorite literary and teaching devices. (By the way, how many of you looked at your Bible just then to see if it was literally "running over" with anything? You didn't.

---

[38] "Metaphor," Learner's Dictionary, accessed June 23, 2018, http://www.learnersdictionary.com/definition/metaphor.

But why not? Because you understood I was not using that phrase in a literal, physical sense, didn't you? Do you begin to see how often we subconsciously understand and process such non-literal figures of speech on a daily basis without so much as a 'second thought?')

Speaking of the phrase "running over" being used in a metaphorical, instead of a literal, physical sense, please take a moment to consider the very popular twenty-third Psalm. It is inundated with figurative, symbolic, non-literal language. God does not force any of us to literally lie down in a literal green pasture. Where exactly is this literal valley of the shadow of death geographically located? Do you truly believe that almighty God needs a literal, wooden, rod and staff to accomplish His purposes? Of course not. But in like fashion, surely the table, anointing, oil, and cup running over in verse five are also not to be taken literally. These, too, are all metaphorically utilized figures of speech used to convey the message of God's providential care for His faithful people. This, just like whenever the Psalms or even Jesus Himself, as in John, Chapter Ten, refer to God's people as "sheep."

A few other biblical examples of the use of this non-literal, metaphorical language in the Old Testament would include, but certainly not be limited to:

- Psalm 18:2: "The Lord is my rock, and my fortress and my deliverer; my God, my strength, in whom I will trust; my shield and the horn of my salvation, my stronghold."

  We know that God is neither a literal rock, fortress, shield, or stronghold, but that these terms are used metaphorically to illustrate His role as protector.

- Proverbs 13:14: "The law of the wise is a fountain of life…" The "fountain of life" is a common metaphor that suggests a continuing source of sustenance and life.

- Isaiah 64:8: "But now, O Lord, You are our Father; We are the clay, and You our potter…" In this metaphor, God is compared to a potter who molds clay, while His followers are the clay which is subject to his design and influence. But obviously we are not literally clay.

In the New Testament, instead of always speaking in terms that were to be taken and understood literally, Jesus – God in the flesh – continued to utilize metaphorical terms to convey His message as well. Jesus referred to Himself symbolically as "bread," "light," and "the vine" (John 6:35, 8:12, and 15:5), while He spoke of His people as "salt," and "branches," and said that if they followed Him they would "never hunger" and "never thirst" (Matthew 5:13, John 15:5, 6:35). Does that latter literally mean that if you as a Christian athlete or worker have ever been hungry or thirsty that the Bible is in error? Of course not. We all understand that Jesus here was speaking figuratively to help His followers to better understand His message.

- **Metonymy:** "A figure of speech in which the name of one thing is used in place of that of another associated with or suggested by it. (Ex.: 'the White House' for 'the President.')"

  As one good brother recently commented, "I always laugh when in the movies [or on television] they say they are going to 'call Washington,' and I get a mental picture of George answering the phone."

  Another everyday example of the usage of this particular type of figure of speech could be seen in a situation wherein a person is asked if they'd like some coffee, and they say, "Sure, I'll take a cup." In this case, "cup" is substituted for, and used in the place of or to refer to, the "coffee" contained within it. Hence, this is an excellent example of metonymy.

Understanding, remembering, and rightly applying especially the final two forms of figures of speech listed above – metaphorical and metonymical - will be both central and crucial to our discussion and understanding of the 'cup' discussion in the upcoming chapters. The thing that we must always understand and keep in mind throughout that discussion about Jesus, is that He, being God in the flesh Who created the mouth to begin with (Exodus 4:11-12), not only spoke and taught utilizing literal terms and language, but that He also understood and utilized figures of speech constantly, consistently, precisely, and whenever necessary, in order to preach, teach, and communicate His message the most effectively. It could well be said that Jesus was the 'Prince of Parables,' the 'Sovereign of Similes,' and the 'Master of the Metaphor.' As proof positive of this very point, please pay very careful attention to what both Jesus and His disciples said of Him near the end of His ministry as recorded in John 16:25-29:

> "'These things I have spoken to you in figurative language; but the time is coming when I will no longer speak to you in figurative language, but I will tell you plainly about the Father. In that day you will ask in My name, and I do not say to you that I shall pray the Father for you; for the Father Himself loves you, because you have loved Me, and have believed that I came forth from God. I came forth from the Father and have come into the world. Again, I leave the world and go to the Father.' His disciples said to Him, 'See, now You are speaking plainly, and using no figure of speech!'"

Apparently, the disciples had become so accustomed to Jesus using "figures language" as He taught them, that it completely surprised and made them quite grateful when He finally began speaking plainly to them.

But why go to such extensive lengths, and spend so much time and effort to explain and document all of this in such great and yet minute detail when it comes to our understanding and this warning to us of how we must be ever-mindful and wary of the differences, between when the Bible is utilizing a figure of speech, as opposed to using language that is to be taken literally? Here's why: Because this one, single, incredibly far-reaching, and potentially devastating element, has been the source of continual and untold confusion leading to many man-made doctrines and misunderstandings, all of which have helped to contribute to the loss of countless thousands, if not millions, of precious and priceless souls. And this failure to differentiate is still one of the main culprits in helping to accomplish the same carnage and confusion when it comes to the 'one cup' discussion, division, and destruction of Christ's disciples' unity today.

Consider: Do you recall the soul-destroying damage done because of this very same failure to discern between when Jesus was using a figure of speech as opposed to language to be taken on a literal or physical level in John 6:35-66? When those disciples misunderstood and mistook His figure of speech regarding eating His flesh and drinking His blood as if He were speaking of literally eating His physical flesh and literally drinking His actual blood, they were completely confused – and why not? Not only would He have been teaching cannibalism to begin with, but mathematically speaking, if Jesus were anywhere around normal height and weight, His actual flesh and blood could not have been used to feed all of His disciples even once around, even if that was what He meant. No wonder they thought it was a hard saying and beyond their understanding. And their resulting confusion subsequently caused them to turn away and walk with Him no more.

Some centuries later, it would seem as if it was probably this very same sort of failure to discern between when Jesus was using a figure of speech to illustrate, as opposed to literal language in John 6:35-66, which helped to cause the therefore completely confused Catholic Church leadership to come up with the phony, misleading, satanically-engineered[39], and man-made false doctrine of 'transubstantiation.'[40]

---

[39] John 8:31-47.
[40] "Transubstantiation," Wikipedia, accessed June 23, 2018, https://en.wikipedia.org/wiki/Transubstantiation.

But that's always what happens whenever any sincerely religious seeker of God or anyone else somehow fails to understand and/or differentiate between when Jesus is using a figure of speech such as a simile, metaphor, metonym, parable and/or etc., versus when He is speaking in plain, literal, and physical terms. Such folks – no matter how good, sincere, or well-intentioned (only with their 'wires crossed' we might say) – then have to create, and continually insist upon implementing their own man-made and devised doctrines, in order to try to make some semblance of sense, of their own metaphorical, versus messed up physical misunderstandings.

As you will recall, even Nicodemus – a good, devoted, sincere, and intelligent religious leader in his own right - struggled mightily with this very same problem. This, as he sought to try to make sense of Jesus' usage of metaphorical language, on a literal, physical, and biological instead of spiritual level, in reference to the necessity of being "born again" before one can enter into the kingdom of God (John 3:1-12). Nor was Nicodemus alone in seeking to try to make some semblance of sense of Jesus' usage of metaphorical as opposed to literal language in the first century (Please see John 4:10-15 and 11:11-14 as examples). Apparently, this lack of understanding and differentiation is not limited to just one or any century, but is particularly prominent in this, our 21st century; and specifically, as it relates to those of the 'one cup' perspective. Let me explain…

Let us consider momentarily – and keeping in mind of course, that some words and/or phrases are used both in a literal and physical, as well as a figurative, metonymic, or metaphorical sense, depending on their different Biblical locations, contexts, and situations – the phrase, "His cross." In Matthew 27:32, Mark 15:21, and John 19:17, the phrase, "His cross," undeniably and inarguably refers to Jesus Christ's literal, physical, wooden cross, upon which He would inevitably be crucified. Please check out those references and see for yourself.

On the other hand, that very same phrase, "his cross," is also used in a very non-literal, non-physical, figurative, metonymical, and/or metaphorical sense, in Matthew 10:38, 16:24;

Mark 8:34; Luke 9:23, and 14:27. (This is not much different than when Christians today either sing or talk about "the cross," when in fact, what they are actually referring to is Jesus and what He accomplished there. The term, "the cross," is a commonly-used and subconsciously processed metaphor or metonym referring to all that Jesus accomplished thereupon… and yet we use and process that figure of speech automatically and without ever even consciously thinking about it. So why so much trouble in doing the same thing with the term "cup," as we do with the term "cross?") Here are those five verses as quoted and taken directly from the New King James Version (**Emphasis** added - DED):

- Matthew 10:38: "And he who does not take ***his cross*** and follow after me is not worthy of me."

- Matthew 16:24: "Then Jesus said to His disciples, 'If anyone desires to come after Me, let him deny Himself, and take up ***his cross***, and follow Me.'"

- Mark 8:34: "When He had called the people to Himself, with His disciples also, He said to them, 'Whoever desires to come after Me, let him deny himself, and take up ***his cross***, and follow Me.'"

- Luke 9:23: "Then He said to them all, 'If anyone desires to come after Me, let him deny Himself, and take up ***his cross*** daily, and follow Me.'"

- Luke 14:27: "And whoever does not bear ***his cross*** and come after Me cannot be My disciple."

Now, can you even begin to imagine the immense sense of panic-stricken confusion and caustic division it would inevitably cause, were some even extremely well-intentioned religious person – and/or more specifically and importantly, one of our very own beloved and blood-bought brethren – to somehow totally fail to recognize and differentiate between when this term, "His cross," is being used in Scripture to define a literal, physical, wooden instrument of torture, and when that same exact term (except of course, for its contextually-demanded capitalization), "his cross," is being used as a metaphorical figure of speech?

What if they then, despite all appeals to its immediate and common-sense context and surroundings, further insisted that this phrase was always and without exception to be taken absolutely literally? And then, what if they should take it still further yet (especially in light of Luke 14:27), and in order to justify and satisfy their own conclusion (which was based solely upon their complete failure to discern the definitive difference between the literal and figurative usage of the phrase), they should develop their own erroneous theology? That theology being, seeing as how they believe that this term in Scripture must always and without exception indicate an absolutely literal cross, that all Christians MUST, without exception, therefore actually and literally carry, an actual and literal, life-sized wooden cross? And that those who don't are summarily lost and automatically doomed to eternal hell due to their disobedience? And therefore, that they (the literal cross-carriers), cannot be in fellowship with their brethren who don't? What would you think of that? Does that make any sense at all to any reader whatsoever?

Might I humbly and lovingly, yet strongly and confidently affirm and suggest to you, the reader, that that is exactly and precisely what our so-called 'one cup' brethren have done, to and with the word "cup." They have failed to differentiate between the times wherein that word is used literally, and the times wherein it is used figuratively or symbolically in reference to something other than itself (such as its contents). This has inevitably led – just as we've seen that it always has - to one's having to come up with all sorts of creative, man-made, but biblically unsustainable viewpoints and perspectives relating to their worship and fellowship.

But don't take my word for it. Please instead check out and study what the Bible says as referenced in the following chapters just like the noble Bereans both would and did (Acts 17:11). Please also objectively pray for godly wisdom and understanding of His will without doubting (James 1:5-6). God bless and good studying.

NOTES

Chapter Seven:

The "Cup" Considered

A couple of points before proceeding any further into the actual study portion of this effort regarding the specific word "cup." First off, please let me briefly reiterate a point previously made… Again, I do not believe, nor can I conceive, of there being any brother or sister on either side of the current division who is seriously seeking to willfully do any harm or damage to the Lord's church. I do not and cannot believe, that there is any brother or sister on either side of this current division who is sincerely seeking to do anything other than to simply learn, understand, and implement what almighty God wants into their worship. If there is, and I am wrong, then surely God will deal with them most appropriately for what they are maliciously and purposefully seeking to do to cut, thwart, harm, divide, and destroy from within, His only begotten Son's, one and only, beautiful and beloved, blood-bought bride.

And secondly; while the Scriptures clearly teach us that there are definitely situations wherein divisions must occur between those brethren in the Lord's church who are doctrinally sound, and those who, instead, insist upon promoting and practicing false and unscriptural doctrines (Romans 16:16-18, 1 Corinthians 11:19), the fact is, that unless it is clearly, concisely, and contextually provable, that either **one communion cup**, or **multiple communion cups**, is a definite departure from Scripture and therefore sinful, then the current division certainly ***IS SINFUL*** (1 Corinthians 1:10-13; Philippians 1:27).

Jesus Himself taught that a kingdom divided against itself will be brought to desolation and will not stand (Matthew 12:25). How desperately sad is it that we, as blood-bought and cleansed children of the living God and members of His Son's one New

Testament church or kingdom, are divided over – of all things – *communion*? This is the divinely-instituted memorial of the one thing that ought most to unite and unify us. Let us allow the apostle Paul's words to our first-century Ephesian brethren, to both ignite and unite us, "to walk worthy of the calling with which [we] were called, with all lowliness and gentleness, with long-suffering, bearing with one another in love, endeavoring to keep the unity of the Spirit in the bond of peace" (Ephesians 4:1-3). Having said these things, let us begin our specific consideration and exploration of the word, "cup."

The word "cup" occurs a grand total of thirty-one times in twenty-eight verses of the New King James translation of the New Testament. And we are going to examine every single one of them in the following pages. This, while exploring the vast majority of them both in depth and at great length, in a loving and comprehensive attempt to seek to acquire the clearest biblical picture and understanding of them that we possibly, humanly can, and thereby, to hopefully help to clear up some of the textual and contextual confusion surrounding these texts relative to our topic, and the ugly, costly, and ungodly division it is causing amongst us.

What you are about to discover, is that both God, Christ, and the Holy Spirit in the New Testament Scriptures, almost always – if not always – used the word "cup," or eventually referred to any literal cup shown to be present, as a metaphor for, or to refer to something else. Do not forget that, ever. Jesus Christ, as well as the directly and divinely-inspired New Testament writers (2 Tim. 3:14-17; 2 Peter 1:16-2:3) typically and almost always referred to a cup – **and even on occasion, when they recorded and context proves that there was a literal, physical cup present** - as a metaphor or symbol for something else other than the actual, literal, lone, physical cup entirely.

And please recall what two of our previously noted definitions of a metaphor are: "A figure of speech, containing an implied comparison, in which a word or phrase ordinarily and primarily used of one thing, is applied to another."[41] "An

---

[41] Webster's New World College Dictionary; Fourth Edition (New York: Marie Butler-Knight, 1999)

object, activity, or idea that is used as a symbol of something else..."[42]

Likewise, please also recall the dictionary definition of, and our comments regarding the figure of speech known as a metonym from Chapter Six: "A figure of speech in which the name of one thing is used in place of that of another associated with or suggested by it. (Ex.: 'the White House' for 'the President.') An everyday example of the usage of this particular type of figure of speech could be seen in a situation wherein a person is asked if they'd like some coffee, and they say, 'Sure, I'll take a cup.' In this case, 'cup' is substituted for, and used in place of, or to refer to, the 'coffee' contained within it. Hence, this is an example of metonymy."

Relative to those two particular figures of speech and their definitions, again: What we are going to find is that Jesus pretty much entirely and exclusively used the term "cup," to represent, point to, illustrate, or to symbolize, something else entirely and other than (and not to refer to) a single, literal, physical "cup" - even when one was obviously present. We shall see this vital point very simply, clearly, plainly, certainly, scripturally, and repeatedly made. It will be undeniable and unmistakable. We shall start by examining those Scriptures in which the word "cup" occurs, but which do not necessarily have anything to do directly with communion...

The first two of our thirty-one New Testament verses which we shall cover that contain the word "cup," are the parallel passages of Matthew 10:42 and Mark 9:41:

- "And whoever gives one of these little ones only a cup of cold water in the name of a disciple, assuredly, I say to you, he shall by no means lose his reward" (Matthew 10:42).

- "For whoever gives you a cup of water to drink in My name, because you belong to Christ, assuredly, I say to you, he will by no means lose his reward" (Mark 9:41).

---

[42] "Metaphor," Learner's Dictionary, accessed June 23, 2018, http://www.learnersdictionary.com/definition/metaphor

If anyone is absolutely adamant and insistent upon these verses making a case for Jesus utilizing only and exclusively literal language when referring to the word "cup" (in order to of course seek to try to sustain their perspective that the word "cup" in Scripture always and exclusively demands one, single, solitary, lone, and literal physical cup), then that would mean that if someone were 'dying of thirst' (either literally or figuratively speaking of course) and was given a cup of cold water, but in their haste and/or deprived state, dropped and shattered it, that to give them a second cup of water - even in order to save their life - would be sinning. This, because as our 'one cup' brethren would contend, when the Scripture uses the word "cup" [singular], then any usage of more than one, under any circumstances, is a sin – no exceptions.

Additionally, and as with all biblical study principles, they must also be consistent. This means that the language in the remainder of those verses must also be taken absolutely literally – with no exceptions as well. And if that is so, then one would only be authorized to give one cup of water to one of those particular people present and mentioned there at that time. (It would also have to be "cold" or else they would be sinning. Tell me, are we going to define an exact temperature where water goes from "warm" or "tepid" to "cold" as well?). Giving even "a cup of cold water" to anyone else other than those folks mentioned there could not be done in compliance with, or obedience to, Jesus' words. And seeing as how all of those particular first-century people present there then have long since passed and gone, then this verse – if one continues to insist upon its having been spoken in absolutely literal language – has no meaning or application for or to us whatsoever.

Does it not make much more common and contextual sense, to understand that Jesus is therein using this "cup" of water, as a metaphorical figure of speech, in order to best convey to all Christians in all ages to come, that no charitable deed, no matter how small, will be forgotten or go unrewarded by God? It certainly does to me.

The third, fourth, fifth, and sixth of our thirty-one occurrences of the word "cup" in the New Testament are found in the parallel accounts of Jesus' words from Matthew 20:20-23 and Mark 10:37-39:

- "Then the mother of Zebedee's sons came to Him with her sons, kneeling down and asking something from Him. And He said to her, 'What do you wish?' She said to Him, 'Grant that these two sons of mine may sit, one on Your right hand and the other on the left, in Your kingdom.' But Jesus answered and said, 'You do not know what you ask. Are you able to drink the cup that I am about to drink, and be baptized with the baptism that I am baptized with?' They said to Him, 'We are able.' So He said to them, 'You will indeed drink My cup, and be baptized with the baptism that I am baptized with; but to sit on My right hand and on My left is not Mine to give, but *it is for those* for whom it is prepared by My Father'" (Matthew 20:20-23).

- "They said to Him, 'Grant us that we may sit, one on Your right hand and the other on Your left, in Your glory.' But Jesus said to them, 'You do not know what you ask. Are you able to drink the cup that I drink, and be baptized with the baptism that I am baptized with?' They said to Him, 'We are able.' So Jesus said to them, 'You will indeed drink the cup that I drink, and with the baptism I am baptized with you will be baptized...'" (Mark 10:37-39).

It should be easily obvious to even the most casual of observers, that Jesus' mentions of drinking "the cup" that He was about to drink as recorded by these two gospel writers, were truly, totally, and thoroughly spoken in the form of a metaphor. They were definitely not any sort of a literal reference to a lone, literal, singular, physical container setting there on a table, such as is used to hold a literal, physical liquid. As we're seeing thus far, Jesus' usage of the word "cup" seldom, if ever, was a direct and literal reference to such...

The seventh, eighth, and ninth of our thirty-one occurrences of the word "cup" in the New Testament are found in the parallel accounts of Jesus' words from Matthew 23:24-28 and Luke 11:39-40:

- "Blind guides, who strain out a gnat and swallow a camel! Woe to you, scribes and Pharisees, hypocrites! For you cleanse the outside of the cup and dish, but inside they are full of extortion and self-indulgence. Blind Pharisee, first cleanse the inside of the cup and dish, that the outside of them may be clean also. Woe to you, scribes and Pharisees, hypocrites! For you are like whitewashed tombs which indeed appear beautiful outwardly, but inside are full of dead *men's* bones and all uncleanness. Even so you also outwardly appear righteous to men, but inside you are full of hypocrisy and lawlessness" (Matthew 23:24-28).

- "Then the Lord said to him, 'Now you Pharisees make the outside of the cup and dish clean, but your inward part is full of greed and wickedness. Foolish ones! Did not He who made the outside make the inside also?'" (Luke 11:39-40).

Question: How does one fill an actual, literal, physical cup and dish to overflowing, with such non-physical, non-tangible, and non-liquid elements as extortion, self-indulgence, greed, and wickedness? Answer: They don't. They can't. It's not possible (any more than actually swallowing a lone and literal camel – which is but just one more of the many and countless examples of Jesus' usage of metaphoric figures of speech to better illustrate and communicate His message). And there is therefore absolutely no possible way on this planet that anyone can honestly read and explore those two passages and then come away having concluded that Jesus was using the word "cup" therein, to signify a lone, literal, singular, physical, liquid-carrying container; or, even more absurdly, that He was actually complaining about how the Pharisees 'did dishes.'

The tenth, eleventh, twelfth, and thirteenth of our thirty-one occurrences of the word "cup" in the New Testament, are found in the parallel accounts of what Jesus is recorded as having prayed to His Father in the Garden of Gethsemane, according to Matthew 26:39 and 42; as well as Mark 14:36 and Luke 22:42:

- "He went a little farther and fell on His face, and prayed, saying, 'O My Father, if it is possible, let this cup pass from Me; nevertheless, not as I will, but as You will'" (Matthew 26:39).

- "Again, a second time, He went away and prayed, saying, 'O My Father, if this cup cannot pass away from Me unless I drink it, Your will be done'" (Matthew 26:42).

- "And He said, 'Abba, Father, all things are possible for You. Take this cup away from Me; nevertheless, not what I will, but what You will'" (Mark 14:36).

- "Saying, 'Father, if it is Your will, take this cup away from Me; nevertheless, not My will, but Yours be done'" (Luke 22:42).

Perhaps there are no greater, stronger, or more powerful passages in all of Scripture than the above when it comes to proving beyond any shadow or sliver of a spiritual doubt, that Jesus consistently and customarily referred to and/or used the word "cup" metaphorically, and not necessarily or typically to refer to a lone, literal, singular, physical, liquid-carrying container. Surely there is no sincere seeker or believer on either side of the 'single/multiple communion cup(s)' debate, who would be so irreverent as to suggest that Jesus Christ took a single, lone, literal, liquid-carrying container into the Garden of Gethsemane with Him the night before He was crucified for the sins of the world (sort of like we might see or take a water bottle with us to some entertainment event today), and then challenged His heavenly Father in prayer to take it from Him... would they? Surely not.

The fourteenth of our thirty-one occurrences of the word "cup" in the New Testament is found in John 18:10-11, and is once again, spoken by none other than Jesus Christ Himself:

- "Then Simon Peter, having a sword, drew it and struck the high priest's servant, and cut off his right ear. The servant's name was Malchus. So Jesus said to Peter, 'Put your sword into the sheath. Shall I not drink the cup which My Father has given Me?'" (John 18:10-11)

Once again, it should be incredibly clear to any sincere observer or reader, that Jesus was only utilizing the word "cup" metaphorically, or as a figure of speech to help illustrate the terrible suffering He was about to undergo in obedience to His Father's will. Surely Jesus did not stop Peter's sword-wielding response so that He could just take a moment to get a swallow of refreshment from a lone and literal "cup" given Him by His heavenly Father here, did He? No. And after all, it is both literally and physically impossible to 'drink a [literal] cup' anyway. One cannot "drink" a solid vessel, but can only drink *from* a solid vessel, and then only that which is a liquid substance from within said solid vessel. Hence, any attempt at an absolutely and all-inclusive literal interpretation of the phrase "drink the cup" in this verse, is seeking to walk on scripturally unsustainable, thin and unmistakable ice. ('Walking on thin ice' of course being a figure of speech and not to be taken literally. Isn't it truly remarkable when you stop and think about it, just how often both we as well as Jesus have used, processed, understood, and communicated clearly and consistently - if not absolutely literally - with them?)

The final four New Testament occurrences of the word "cup," which we shall examine prior to looking at those thirteen occurrences of the term which are specifically related to the celebration of communion, are all four found in the Book of Revelation. And as per the usual, not one, single, solitary one of them, is referring to one, lone, single, solitary, literal, or physical "cup." They are all instead, used symbolically or metaphorically, as representative of something other than such a lone and literal "cup." These are found in Revelation 14:9-10, 16:19, 17:4, and 18:4-6:

- "Then a third angel followed them, saying with a loud voice, 'If anyone worships the beast and his image, and receives *his* mark on his forehead or on his hand, he himself shall also drink of the wine of the wrath of God, which is poured out full strength into the cup of His indignation'" (Revelation 14:9-10).

- "Now the great city was divided into three parts, and the cities of the nations fell. And great Babylon was remembered before God, to give her the cup of the wine of the fierceness of His wrath" (Revelation 16:19).

- "The woman was arrayed in purple and scarlet, and adorned with gold and precious stones and pearls, having in her hand a golden cup full of abominations and the filthiness of her fornication" (Revelation 17:4).

- "And I heard another voice from heaven saying, 'Come out of her, my people, lest you share in her sins, and lest you receive of her plagues. For her sins have reached to heaven, and God has remembered her iniquities. Render to her just as she rendered to you, and repay her double according to her works; in the cup which she has mixed, mix double for her'" (Revelation 18:4-6).

It should be incredibly obvious – without any explanation from me in any form – to even the most casual of readers, that not one single one of the four above-cited references, has anything whatsoever to do with a lone, literal, singular, physical container, even though the word "cup" is used in every single one of them.

Now, by this time, you as the reader might well be thinking, 'Why on earth, in a book supposedly devoted to the biblical discussion of whether or not we should be using one or multiple cups or containers in the celebration of communion in order to be obedient and right with God, has Doug now spent so much time, effort, ink, and energy, dealing with so many verses which seemingly have nothing at all to do with communion?' And the answer is: 'Because they have everything to do with it!' And here's how...

One of the biggest and certainly most eternally-costly mistakes that many misled people make when seeking to study a specific topic or subject in God's holy word, is to totally disregard or fail to take into account that the God of the Bible is the God of consistency and patterns (Exodus 25:9, 40; Acts 7:44; 2 Timothy 1:13; Hebrews 8:1-5). And that that is never going to change – ever (Psalm 103, 119:89; Malachi 3:6; Hebrews 6:17-18, 13:8; Proverbs 24:21-22). It is no coincidence that this same God who began His creation of the new physical world in the Old Testament by utilizing both water and His Holy Spirit working in close and intimate proximity (Genesis 1:1-2), also uses water and His Spirit working in close and intimate proximity to create the new spiritual man in Christ as outlined in the New Testament (John 3:3-5; Acts 2:38-41; 2 Corinthians 5:17).

Nor is it some cosmic coincidence, chance circumstance, or unforeseen happenstance, that just as one had to get into the ark in order to be saved - thus being separated from the sinful world all around them by the water - that salvation today is accomplished according to the same divine pattern of hearing, obeying, and complying with God's commandments; i.e., that one has to get "into Christ" (Romans 6:1-11; Galatians 3:26-27) in order to be saved, being thus separated from the sinful world by the waters of Christian baptism (1 Peter 3:18-22).

Our God is **the** God of complete consistency, accuracy, and definite, definitive, and divinely-inspired patterns. Therefore, it is nothing less than absolutely imperative that in a study of such a 'hot button' word or topic as the word "cup," and what it means and can mean to our current discussion, division, and the eternally far-reaching implications, complications, and consequences that it both can and does have, that we look at each and every occurrence of the word in Scripture that we possibly can in order to see what divinely-inspired and consistent patterns we can discover as to its usage therein.

God's divine pattern to this point, from each and every one of the eighteen occurrences of the word "cup" that we have thus far covered, should be nothing short of crystal clear, and utterly and completely undeniable: The word "cup," in the New Testament, has been repeatedly, consistently, and continually used metonymically, metaphorically, symbolically, and not to in any sense whatsoever, indicate or literally refer to and/or insist on, one, lone, literal, drinking container – period.

The reason this divine truth is so critically and vitally essential to understand and accept as we head headlong into our study of all of the other occurrences of the word in the New Testament, wherein it is used in direct reference to the celebration of communion each and every Sunday in the Lord's church (Acts 20:7), is because this ever-consistent God's word, is also, obviously, utterly consistent, just as He is.

Jesus Christ Himself, in commenting on this perfectly harmonious accuracy, agreement, and consistency within and throughout the word of God, said that "the Scripture cannot be broken" (John 10:35). In other words, Scripture cannot contradict itself. How or what a word or phrase is typically used for or means in Scripture in one place - unless there is an obvious contextual difference or inconsistency - it is typically used for, means, or is defined as in other places.

The fact that "the Bible is its own best interpreter" is the elemental and monumental truth which so many misled denominationalists, due to their own man-made definitions, miss to their own eternal demise. For example, they rightly contend that one must 'call on the name of the Lord' to be saved (Acts 2:21; Romans 10:9-13), but then define that phrase to mean saying a prayer. But God's definition of that same phrase elsewhere in Scripture has nothing whatsoever to do with saying the so-called 'sinner's prayer,' but is something done only and exclusively through being baptized to wash away, or for the forgiveness of, their sins (Acts 22:16; 2:38).

I fear that the same thing might tragically be true, for any and all who would willfully choose to fail to see, discern, and accept the truth about how our God of consistency, consistently used the word "cup" metaphorically everywhere else in the New Testament, as we continue on now into our discussion of the communion texts…

NOTES

Chapter Eight:
The Communion

The word "cup" is often and indeed used in our vernacular to indicate a lone, literal, singular, physical, touchable object. This, just as the words "cross," "sheep," "lamb" and/or other words like them are used to indicate or refer to other literal, physical, tangible, and touchable things. And just as the words indicating those literal objects are all also often used metaphorically to represent or symbolize something other than themselves in the Scriptures, thus far, in eighteen out of thirty-one occurrences of the word "cup" (that's nearly sixty percent of said occurrences) which we have examined in the New Testament before ever even approaching those last thirteen occurrences which are located in texts specifically related to communion, we have indisputably seen that that word "cup" was used symbolically, metaphorically, metonymically, and not literally, in every single one of them. We have inarguably seen and studied how that term "cup" was repeatedly used as a figure of speech, to symbolize or stand for something else and other than itself, and not to refer to a lone, literal, singular, physical cup, in every single one of those eighteen occurrences.

The word "cup," in those cases we have covered thus far, was always and without exception used to simply signify, symbolize, represent, refer to, or to illustrate the complete range of contents, ingredients, or components, contained in whatever particular event, process, or experience was being described, defined, discussed, illustrated, or alluded to at the time. But, what about the other thirteen New Testament occurrences of the word "cup" regarding its relationship to our weekly communion celebration? Not surprisingly at all - seeing as how we serve, worship, seek, and celebrate the God of absolute and utter consistency and patterns – we shall see this same truth made even more boldly and abundantly clear.

There are five more occurrences of the word "cup" in the four gospel accounts which we shall now explore; all five of which are directly involved with our Lord's institution of what we commonly refer to as "communion" (1 Corinthians 10:16). The first two of these which we shall examine are found in Matthew 26:27 and Mark 14:23:

- "Then He took the cup, and gave thanks, and gave it to them, saying, 'Drink from it, all of you'" (Matthew 26:27).

- "Then He took the cup, and when He had given thanks He gave it to them, and they all drank from it" (Mark 14:23).

Now, admittedly, at first glance, and without any further regard for their textual and/or contextual surroundings - that is to say, were these two verses to somehow get plucked up, pulled out, and summarily separated from all of the other relevant and/or surrounding passages addressing the same subject - it is, on the surface, quite easy to see how some might easily take them to indicate that Jesus and His disciples all drank from the same "cup" that night, and to therefore conclude that we must also.

But, have we not learned anything whatsoever about such a sadly inadequate study technique from our denominational friends and neighbors? Is this not the same sort of egregious theological study error which so many of them so often fall into? Is this not exactly how they arrive at their biblically contrarian conclusion that baptism is not at all necessary for salvation?

By plucking up John 3:16 out of John 3:1-36; by pulling Acts 16:30-31 out and away from Acts 16:32-34; and by separating Romans 10:9-10 from Romans 10:11-17 – as well as disconnecting these specific biblical texts from all of the rest of those texts which teach us so implicitly that baptism is absolutely essential for salvation (such as Mark 16:16, 1 Peter 3:21, and others) – is precisely how they arrive at, and are then forced to defend, such a biblically unsustainable position. My beloved brethren; we simply dare not, cannot, must not and will not therefore, allow ourselves to get caught up, swallowed up, and then swept away into following in their footsteps.

As the apostle Paul instructed Timothy to do in 2 Timothy 2:15, so must we also 'study to show ourselves approved to God, as workmen that need not to be ashamed, rightly dividing the word of truth.' And so, let us explore that first text in much greater and more widespread detail:

> Matthew 26:26-29 states: "And as they were eating, Jesus took bread, blessed and broke *it,* and gave *it* to the disciples and said, 'Take, eat; this is My body.' ²⁷ Then He took the cup, and gave thanks, and gave *it* to them, saying, 'Drink from it, all of you. ²⁸ For this is My blood of the new covenant, which is shed for many for the remission of sins. ²⁹ But I say to you, I will not drink of this fruit of the vine from now on until that day when I drink it new with you in My Father's kingdom.'"

First off, please notice that in verse twenty-six, Jesus said that the bread which He broke and gave to them was His body. Obviously, He was not seeking to imply or indicate that that loaf of bread was His actual, literal, physical flesh and bone body. He was, once again, as He so often did, speaking metaphorically.

Notice that He next then "took the cup," "gave thanks," "gave *it* to them," and told them to "drink from it." Yes, Jesus did indeed take up a lone, literal, singular, physical, "cup," "gave thanks," and "gave to them" (The italicized word "*it*" was not in the original Greek there in that phrase, but was added for flow and readability when translated into English. That's why it's italicized – See notes on "Format" in the front of your Bible), telling them to "drink from '*it*.'" Now, the solution to coming to a common understanding and becoming of one mind (Philippians 1:27-2:2) regarding the entire issue at hand here, has everything to do with accurately determining precisely what the "*it*" was that Jesus was referring to near the very end of verse twenty-seven. While it is obvious and inarguable that it was indeed a literal cup which He initially took up, He makes it even more obviously and inarguably clear that the "cup" was to be considered as a metaphor or metonym for what the "it" was which they literally drank and drank from - what the "it" was for which He had actually given thanks. And that was the "it" which most resembled His blood (verse 28) – the "it" which the "cup" literally contained. And that was "the fruit of the vine" which He would not "drink of" again until He could do so in His "Father's kingdom," according to none other than the Lord Jesus Christ Himself (verses 28-29).

Remember; the Bible is its own best interpreter. It is its own best dictionary and definer. Jesus Christ Himself, the living "Word became flesh and dwelt among us" (John 1:14), both clarified, verified, and identified, exactly what the all important and literal "it" was: ***to*** which He referred; ***for*** which He gave thanks; and ***from*** which He told them all to drink - and it certainly wasn't the "cup." He Himself confirmed it was "the fruit of the vine" - the cup's contents. Brother Guy N. Woods further explains and confirms:[43]

> Obviously, Jesus did not tell his disciples to drink the container; He did not give thanks for the container; "the cup" which He gave thanks for, "the cup" which He bade the disciples to drink, was that which the literal cup contained – the fruit of the vine. Thus, by metonymy [the container "for the thing contained" – Webster's Collegiate Dictionary], our Lord used "the cup" to signify what it contained, [what the contents were] the fruit of the vine. This, the context clearly shows: It is first said that the Lord took "the cup," gave thanks for "the cup," and instructed the disciples to drink **it**. But later, when alluding to that which He took, [that] for which He gave thanks, and [that from] which He told the disciples to drink, He said, "I will not drink henceforth of this fruit

---

[43] Guy N. Woods, "Questions And Answers; Open Forum," *Freed-Hardeman College Lectures*, (1976) 209-210.

of the vine until that day when I drink it new with you in My Father's kingdom."

Thus, "the cup" of the first sentence (verse 27), becomes "this fruit of the vine" in the last sentence (verse 29). In effect, the Lord said, "By the 'cup' I mean, 'this fruit of the vine';" the one cup (container) advocates say, 'by the cup' we mean the container!"

The Lord regarded "the cup" as the contents; opposers of individual communion containers regard "the cup" as the vessel. They are thus in hopeless conflict with the Lord in this matter. The two positions are beyond reconciliation. The cup, defined by the Lord, is that which it contains, and the vessel is without significance; those who contend for one container, transfer the significance to the container, thus differing sharply with the Lord on what "the cup" is. Inasmuch as "the cup," by our Lord's definition, is "the fruit of the vine," it follows that when we use the fruit of the vine (juice of the grape), we have but one cup, regardless of how many containers may be used to distribute it!

We see this same, exact, scriptural truth very clearly and concisely conveyed and confirmed yet once again, as we conduct an honest, objective, and in-depth examination and investigation of the second and parallel Scripture reference as cited above.

Mark 14:22-25 states: "And as they were eating, Jesus took bread, blessed and broke *it,* and gave *it* to them and said, 'Take, eat; this is My body.' [23] Then He took the cup, and when He had given thanks He gave *it* to them, and they all drank from it. [24] And He said to them, 'This is My blood of the new covenant, which is shed for many. [25] Assuredly, I say to you, I will no longer drink of the fruit of the vine until that day when I drink it new in the kingdom of God.'"

The word "cup" in this passage, although obviously initially referring to a literal, physical, liquid-containing vessel, cannot be the literal, physical "it," or element that is being emphasized by the text when it states that "they all drank from it" - except and/or unless the word "cup" is simply being utilized as a metaphorical figure of speech pointing to its contents, just as the Lord had used the figure on so many other (previously covered in this book) occasions. The Lord again made this very point incredibly and unmistakably clear when He specifically told them (and us by extension) that "it" (verse 23), was "the fruit of the vine" (verse 25), from which they "all drank" (verse 23), and for which "He had given thanks" (verse 23).

Now, over the years, some ardent supporters of the 'one cup or else' insistence have also sought to convince us that there were three elements of importance instituted in the 'Lord's Supper' that night, as opposed to just two. They claim that the three were the bread, the fruit of the vine, and the cup. Recently, it has been reported to me that this reasoning is making some sort of resurgence in some areas of our beloved brotherhood today. But it is still just as erroneous and misleading now as it's always been; and just as erroneous and misleading as it was when brother Elmer Moore very thoroughly addressed and adequately thwarted it in a debate with a 'one cup' brother some three decades ago when he stated the following:[44]

> **The Real Issue**: Many times side issues cloud the *real* issue in a discussion. I hope to avoid this by stating what I believe to be the *real issue*. The issue actually involves two basic questions. First, is the *number* of drinking vessels significant, or is the number essential or merely incidental? Secondly, does the drinking vessel signify anything pertaining to the *design* or *purpose* of the Lords Supper?

---

[44] "Moore-Wade Debate on Communion Cups," Old Paths Advocate, Elmer Moore and Ronny Wade, accessed June 23, 2018, http://www.oldpathsadvocate.org/public/php-scripts/debates/debate2.php

The Design or Purpose of the Lords Supper: The New Testament declares that the purpose of the Lord's Supper is that of a memorial. Jesus said, "This do in remembrance of me" (Lk 22:19; 1 Cor 11:24). The Lord's Supper is a *memorial,* a remembrance of the death of our Lord till He comes again. Allow me to state what I believe is a fundamental principle that I don't believe my brother will deny. *Whatever is essential to the keeping of this memorial must have some specific bearing on the design or purpose of that memorial.* Thus the "bread" which is a fair representation of the body of our Lord, and the "cup the fruit of the vine" which is a fair representation of the blood of the Lord, have a definite bearing on the design of that memorial, and are thus essential. However, the drinking vessel has no significance whatever to the death of our Lord any more than the "table" upon which the elements were placed and the plate used to serve the bread.

...Our Lord used metaphorical language, declaring that "one thing is another" (see Dungan's *Hermeneutics, p. 253,* and Bullinger's *Figures of Speech,* pp. 738-741). Note the language; He took bread and said, "Take eat; this (bread) is my body." He took a cup and said take and drink, for "this (cup) is my blood of the covenant" represented by the fruit of the vine. Friends, if you can see that the word "this" in v. 26 refers back to "bread" in the same passage, why do you have difficulty in seeing that the word "this" in v. 28 refers back to "cup" in v. 27? Note also how Jesus explained His own metaphor by declaring what the "cup" was. He said, "I say unto you I will not drink henceforth of this *fruit of the vine (my emp.).* . . "(v. *29). Our Lord identified the cup. He said it was the fruit of the vine,* and that it was a fair representation of His blood.

The Drinking Vessel Signifies Nothing: That a vessel or container is necessary to contain liquid is not denied. However, the number is immaterial. The drinking vessel has no greater significance than does "the table" (Lk 22:21) upon which the elements were placed, or the upper room where the supper was instituted and later observed (Lk 22:12; Acts 20:8). We must exercise caution that we do not emphasize a matter that the Lord does not emphasize. This is just as bad as failing to make a matter important that the Lord had made important! Brethren, we must realize that it is as bad to *bind* where the Lord has not bound as it is to *loose* where He has not loosed. Either extreme is wrong, and the one as bad as the other.

...Paul declared in I Corinthians 10:16 that the "cup of blessing was a communion of the blood of Christ," and that the "bread was a communion of the body of Christ." Do you not see that there are two elements of significance, which are the bread which is a fair representation of His body and the cup, the fruit of the vine, which is a fair representation of His blood?

...Paul and Luke were using the figure of speech of metonomy, i.e., the container for the contents. The record indicates that they were to "divide" the cup and "drink" it. Thayer on page 533 states, "by metonomy of the container for the contained, the contents of the cup, what is offered to be drunk" (Lk 22:20b; 1 Cor 11:28sq). Both of these writers are talking about the *contents*. Obviously, then, in whatever sense the "cup" is the New Testament it is the contents and not the container.

However, and in addition to all of that, there is perhaps no more pointed, poignant, powerful, or persuasive passage or portion of Scripture when it comes to the whole 'one cup' position being completely unsustainable from a biblical standpoint, than the New Testament text which contains our final three occurrences of the word "cup" in the four gospel accounts. For any and all who would honestly and objectively explore and take to heart what it actually states, it is simply devastating to, and completely destroys the entire "singular communion cup only" doctrine, which is rooted in a total misunderstanding of metaphorical language relative to our Lord's repeated usage of, and reference to, the word "cup." That passage is Luke 22:17-20 which states:

> "Then He took the cup, and gave thanks, and said, 'Take this and divide *it* among yourselves; [18] for I say to you, I will not drink of the fruit of the vine until the kingdom of God comes.' [19] And He took bread, gave thanks and broke *it,* and gave *it* to them, saying, 'This is My body which is given for you; do this in remembrance of Me.' [20] Likewise He also *took* the cup after supper, saying, 'This cup *is* the new covenant in My blood, which is shed for you.'"

As in previously examined Scriptures, what we will again discover here, is that Jesus did not deviate from His pattern of referring to a "cup" (even though there was a literal cup present) as a symbol, or to signify something other than the literal cup itself (in this case, the fruit of the vine which the cup contained), just as He had used the word "cup" symbolically to signify or represent something other than a literal cup on so many other occasions. After all, anything else would be a complete deviation from His and His heavenly Father's divine pattern of usage. Let us now break that passage down and see this truth revealed firsthand.

To begin with, just as in the two passages explored immediately prior to this one, we see Jesus speaking metaphorically or symbolically, using the bread merely as an illustration of, or allusion to, His physical body.

But now, moving into our exploration of the other and our main element under discussion, verse seventeen states in part, "Then He took the cup, and gave thanks, and said, 'Take this...'" Now, in order for the Lord's church to truly come to a common and unified understanding and conclusion on communion, we must determine exactly, precisely, and definitively, just what the word "this" refers to in that text. You see, **IF,** by the word "this," Jesus is only, exclusively, literally referring to that one, singular, literal cup and nothing else – as I believe so many of our so-called 'one-cup' brethren would insist upon – then there are several, biblically unsustainable and irreconcilable problems that such a position always and inevitably creates.

The first problem surfaces immediately upon the completion of a reading of the entirety of verse seventeen: "Then He took the cup, and gave thanks, and said, 'Take this and divide *it* among yourselves...' If the word "this," as well as the later added for flow word "*it*," literally refer to the lone, literal, singular physical cup and nothing else, then how did the twelve disciples "divide *it*" – the cup – among themselves as Jesus commanded? Did they drop it on the floor in an attempt to smash or thus "divide *it*" down into a dozen different pieces – one for each of them? Did they reach for a saw, a sword, a chisel, or a hammer to thus "divide *it*" – the cup – among themselves as Jesus commanded? Again, if the word "this," as well as the word "*it*" in this verse, literally refer to one, lone, literal, singular cup and nothing else, then how exactly did the twelve disciples "divide *it*" – the cup – among themselves as Jesus commanded? And, once they thus divided (smashed/sawed/cut/split/chiseled or however they divided) the literal cup down into a dozen pieces, how did they then actually drink from its shattered or separated shards or fragments anyway?

Additionally, did Jesus then miraculously repair and/or re-attach it back together like He did with Malchus and his ear?[45] He must have if He was actually referring to the one, lone, literal "cup" when He told His disciples to "Take this and divide *it* among yourselves" and they obeyed Him, because in verse twenty we read that after supper, "He also *took* the cup." It does not say He took 'a cup,' or 'another cup,' but "the cup." If one is so adamant and insistent on there being only one cup (due to the singularity of the term as seen in these Scriptures) that they are willing to define, divide, and then discriminate and insist on those divisions within and amongst the fellowship of the Lord's disciples over it, then they must also be prepared to

---

[45] Luke 22:49-51; John 18:10.

defend that "the cup" which Jesus took after supper (as seen in verse twenty), is also, the same, exact, lone and literal "cup" which we also see in verse seventeen; the same cup which the disciples apparently somehow divided or broke apart upon Jesus' command to do so, but which Jesus apparently then had to have miraculously put back together or re-assembled somehow... (?).

A second irreconcilable issue with insisting on taking Jesus' words, "Take this and divide it among yourselves" in verse seventeen to mean that He was absolutely referring to that lone physical cup in an exclusively literal fashion (and not to symbolically or metonymically refer to its contents), is that such a perspective puts the defender thereof in a completely untenable and biblically indefensible position (as previously discussed regarding other, similar communion texts). It puts those who would promote such a position in a state of hopeless contradiction to the words of the Lord Jesus Christ Himself. This is very easily seen, validated, and forever settled[46] by verse eighteen, wherein Jesus specifically defines and clarifies exactly what the "this" and "it" was, which He wanted for them to "take... and divide... among themselves" – "the fruit of the vine." He said so Himself. See for yourself right there in your own Bible.

A third problem that arises with a completely exclusive insistence on the phrase "the cup" and any of the other references to it in these passages being taken absolutely and in all circumstances literally is this: Have you ever noticed that the phrase 'one cup,' never, actually, literally occurs anywhere in the Scriptures? That's right. Look it up in/on your favorite Bible reference, app, website, or computer program; it's not there... anywhere. So, if we're going to get all absolutely literal (and don't get me wrong, I'm all about being strictly, utterly, and absolutely literal when it comes to studying and learning God's word... **EXCEPT** when it is just as contextually clear, provable, obvious, and unquestionable that a specific Scripture is instead using some figure of speech to teach us what God wants, like here), Jesus never says 'one cup.' But what He does say is, "*this* cup." In fact, if one is still going to insist on an

---

[46] Psalm 119:89.

absolutely literal interpretation of even the divinely-inspired usage of figures of speech, then Scripture only instructs and refers to Jesus' disciples taking the same exact cup Jesus used: "***this*** cup." And it does so not only here in Luke 22:20, but another three times throughout 1 Corinthians 11:25-27 just as we shall soon see.

What's the point? Simply this: that those who would so adamantly insist on using only one communion cup based on what they say they see in these scriptural texts, that they are willing to condemn and divide from those of their blood-bought brethren who simply use multiple cups in their communion celebration, desperately need to come to understand that they themselves are not really following the absolutely literal interpretation method which they pride themselves on using, while at the same time condemning others for not so doing. **For if they did, then they would have to literally insist on using only that same, one, lone, literal, exact, "*this* cup," which the Lord Jesus Christ held in His very own and about to be pierced hand that evening.** That's right. The one He must have somehow miraculously fixed after His disciples "divided it" so He could take it up again after supper (?).

The 'one cup' brother engaged with brother Moore in the immediately afore-referenced and cited debate, in seeking to defend his biblically indefensible 'one-cup' perspective, made the following statement:

> "First of all the drinking vessel is named and specified (Mt 26:27); let our brother deny it. If it is specified and named (as it is) then we can conclude that it is taught explicitly (i.e. "clearly developed with all its elements apparent"). The number is not incidental because Jesus specified the number (i.e. "a cup," "the cup"). Paul specified "this cup," "that cup."

Okay; following his own line of reasoning then: First of all, the drinking vessel is named and specified, he is correct; However, Jesus specifically named and specified only "***this*** cup" (***emphasis*** mine; Luke 22:20; 1 Corinthians 11:25, 26, and 27); let *this* brother deny it. If **that** cup which Jesus held in His hand that night is specified and named (as it is) then we can conclude that it is taught explicitly (i.e. "clearly developed with all its elements apparent"). **Which** particular cup to be used is not incidental because Jesus specified exactly **which** cup He meant (i.e. "***this*** cup,"). Paul specified "***this*** cup" as well.

So why did/does not this 'one cup' brother and all of those who pay lip service to adherence to his reasoning, not actually follow his reasoning in reality? That is to say, why did he/do they not see that Jesus named and specified exactly **which** cup ("***this***" cup), meaning that that particular cup and no other is taught explicitly, and that that particular "this cup" Jesus literally and specifically named and referred to is not therefore incidental in our communion celebrations?

According to his very own reasoning process, absolutely no other cup, other than the one Jesus specifically used, named, and specifically specified will ever do for our communion celebrations. And to use any other is to sin so as to go to eternal hell. After all, that is exactly and explicitly where this 'one cup' brother's reasoning inevitably, invariably, and in all reality always leads anyone who would truly claim to follow it. Look it up for yourself. Did not Jesus say "***this*** cup" in those texts? Yes. He did.

Now, can you even begin to imagine someone today, not only seriously adopting, but also taking that reasoning to such an absolute extreme that they would insist that anyone not using that same, one, "***this*** cup" which Jesus used that night, was going to be eternally condemned... when even they themselves were not physically and/or literally able to do that which they insisted others had to do in order to be saved? You say, "That's ridiculous!" You know what? You're absolutely correct. But such is the confusion and chaos one creates whenever they fail to discern the difference between when God is using figurative, metonymical, or metaphoric and symbolic, as opposed to literal language, references, and terminology.

However, and by contrast, if we understand Jesus' usage of the figure of speech known as metonymy; if we rightly divide the word by discerning the all-important difference between language usage in which one term is being used to refer to something associated with or implied by it instead of always used in reference to itself or the literal element itself present; then Luke 22:17-20 makes perfectly clear and simple sense. And it definitely does NOT, in any way, shape, or form, insist on, nor require, the usage of only 'one cup' in our communion celebrations each Sunday. It would much quicker and more appropriately require the usage of that one, particular, "***this*** cup" that Jesus used that night than it would just any old, singular, modern-day cup, should one still choose to fail to differentiate between literal and figurative language. But when one does differentiate, here's what they can and should easily understand from Luke 22:17-20:

> Jesus took the [*literal*] cup, and gave thanks, and said, "Take this [*cup full of fruit of the vine*] and divide *it* [*the fruit of the vine*] among yourselves; for I say to you, I will not drink of the fruit of the vine until the kingdom of God comes." And He took bread, gave thanks and broke *it,* and gave *it* to them, saying, "This is My body which is given for you; do this in remembrance of Me." Likewise He also *took* the [*literal*] cup after supper, saying, "This cup [the word 'cup' here symbolizing, or being used metonymically as a figure of speech to refer to what was inside of it, i.e., the fruit of the vine] *is* the new covenant in My blood, which is shed for you."

So then, how would they, the disciples, at that point have obeyed Jesus' command and divided the fruit of the vine (not the literal cup) among themselves in order to "drink from it" (the fruit of the vine) just as we saw that Jesus commanded them to do according to Matthew 26:27 and Mark 14:23? What is the most logical, common-sense, and biblically-necessary inference here? Is it not that they would have had to have 'divided it' down among themselves in much the same fashion as we would do today at any meal wherein there was a pitcher or container full of any liquid which must be divided down amongst any family at any table? By pouring it out into their own, personal, individual cups, from the one initially containing the liquid? By doing exactly the same thing, and following exactly the same process as we do in preparation for, and in the partaking of, the fruit of the vine in our communion celebration each Sunday? By pouring the fruit of the vine out of the one, lone, original, singular container it was initially packaged and purchased in, and dividing it down amongst ourselves by way of its being poured out and into our own, individual communion cups from whence we drink it – the fruit of the vine which resembles and represents His shed blood – and thus commune with the Christ and with one another in complete and obedient compliance with His commandments? Yes.

If one truly understands that whenever Jesus spoke in reference to the literal cup there on the table, that He referred to it figuratively, and only to point to its literal and blood-resembling contents – the fruit of the vine – then understanding all of these gospel passages becomes incredibly simple, easy, and easy to 'stand together' on. This, as we would point out by simply replacing his references to the cup, with the actual words, "fruit of the vine," which Jesus Himself said that He meant:

- Matthew 26:27-29: "Then He took the cup, and gave thanks, and gave *[the fruit of the vine]* to them, saying, 'Drink from it, all of you. ²⁸ For this *[fruit of the vine]* is My blood of the new covenant, which is shed for many for the remission of sins. ²⁹ But I say to you, I will not drink of this fruit of the vine from now on until that day when I drink it new with you in My Father's kingdom.'"

- Mark 14:23-25: "Then He took the cup, and when He had given thanks He gave *[the fruit of the vine]* to them, and they all drank from *[the fruit of the vine]*. ²⁴ And He said to them, 'This *[fruit of the vine]* is My blood of the new covenant, which is shed for many. ²⁵ Assuredly, I say to you, I will no longer drink of the fruit of the vine until that day when I drink it new in the kingdom of God.'"

- Luke 22:17-18, 20: "Then He took the cup, and gave thanks, and said, 'Take this *[fruit of the vine]* and divide *[this fruit of the vine]* among yourselves; ¹⁸ for I say to you, I will not drink of the fruit of the vine until the kingdom of God comes.' ...Likewise He also *took* the cup after supper, saying, 'This *[fruit of the vine] is* the new covenant in My blood, which is shed for you.'"

Now, viewing those three texts in close succession, some might be inclined to think that Matthew and Mark's accounts somehow seem to contradict Luke's account. However, this is just a simple misunderstanding of Scripture, the same way as when we consider the thieves on the crosses. In Matthew and Mark's account of the crucifixion, BOTH thieves are reported to have blasphemed Jesus (Matthew 27:44, Mark 15:32). But according to Luke's account, only one did (Luke 23:39-41). So, which is correct? All three. And here's why: When we assemble all three of these accounts together (like pieces of a puzzle are assembled together to get the entire 'picture' instead of just relying on a small piece or snapshot to try to see the overall picture), what is the most logical, common-sense, and biblically-necessary inference here? Is it not that we come to rightly 'connect the dots' and thus understand that early on in the crucifixion event (the time frame within which the events as reported by Matthew and Mark apparently took place), both thieves blasphemed Jesus just as reported? However, apparently as the hours passed, one of the thieves, watching how Jesus responded to it all, had a change of heart and came to understand and respond to Jesus more positively, just as Luke records. Hence, all three accounts, though differing, are completely true – WHEN assembled together correctly.

The same is true with the three gospel accounts as seen bulleted immediately above as they relate to "the cup" and its contents. When assembled together correctly, they make simple, perfect, and completely harmonious biblical sense:

> Then He took the (literal) cup, and gave thanks, and gave *[the fruit of the vine]* to them and said, "Take *[this fruit of the vine]* and divide

> *it* among yourselves. Drink from *[this fruit of the vine]*, all of you. And they all drank from *[the fruit of the vine]*.

There is absolutely no insistence or implication there whatsoever of the usage of only 'one cup or else.' In fact, quite to the contrary. Christ's very own 'inner circle' of disciples/apostles, that very night, divided the fruit of the vine down amongst themselves and then drank it.

And so, with all due diligence, love, respect, and humility, might I therefore say, that if indeed it is true (as so many of our 'one cup' brethren seem to have concluded), that using more than one cup during the communion celebration Jesus was instituting that evening *is* indeed a sin... then the very Son of God Himself both sinned (which we know from Scripture that He certainly did not do – Hebrews 4:14-16), **and**, commanded, promoted, and supported His disciples' sinning that evening as well, by instructing them to "divide it" – the fruit of the vine - down amongst themselves (and obviously into their own individual containers), therefore condemning Himself even more by insisting on their sinning (Romans 1:32).

Additionally, isn't it therefore true that for anyone to condemn, refer to as heretics, or to see as unsaved, those who would simply make use of multiple containers in this celebration instead of just the one, is to condemn, refer to as heretics, and view as unsaved, Jesus' apostles, and yes, even Jesus Himself? And what Christian would really want to separate themselves from Jesus and His disciples? But to insist on separating ones' self from any and all 'multiple cup' groups, would have to mean separating from this one which divided the fruit of the vine down amongst themselves before drinking it in compliance with their Lord's commandments...

NOTES

Chapter Nine:

The Corinthians

Thus far in our study we have discussed, dissected, explored, and examined in great detail, a grand total of some twenty-three of the thirty-one occurrences of the word "cup" as seen in the New King James Version of the New Testament. In the first eighteen of those thirty-one occurrences which we noted and studied in Chapter Seven, we saw that the word "cup" was very seldom used to refer to a lone, literal, physical cup; and that even on the rare occasion where a literal cup was mentioned, that it was also, in that same passage, soon thereafter referred to metaphorically or metonymically as well, to either represent, emphasize, symbolize, illustrate, or point to something other than, but still related to, itself – things such as its contents or what the specific situation under consideration would actually involve or contain.

In the next five of those thirty-one occurrences which we covered and studied in Chapter Eight – all having to do specifically with the Lord's institution of His church's weekly communion celebration[47] – we saw these same, exact, and obvious truths once again in evidence. But certainly the one thing we did NOT see in any of those twenty-three divinely-inspired New Testament usages of the word "cup" which we have covered to this point, as divinely-dictated by this very pattern-oriented, pattern-providing, and pattern-instituting God, was any sign of a legitimate command, example, or necessary inference; or any emphasis, instruction, or insistence whatsoever upon the absolute essentiality of all of Jesus' disciples all having to use the same, one, lone, literal, physical communion container in their weekly observance of communion or else be

---

[47] 1 Corinthians 11:26; Acts 20:7.

condemned eternally. It just, simply, wasn't there, just as we saw.

Therefore, we are literally left with no other sound, spiritual, biblical choice, but to rightly conclude that any continued, all-out and 'no exceptions' insistence upon an absolutely literal and singular interpretation of a metaphorically-utilized word like "cup" in the Scriptures, only takes us further away from God and Christ's intended purpose, meaning, practice, and unifying instruction, instead of any closer to any of them. It should additionally therefore, come as no surprise to anyone, that as we consider the final eight New Testament occurrences of the word "cup" as contained in the apostle Paul's divinely-inspired instructions and commandments to the congregation of the Lord's church which worked and worshipped in the first century city of Corinth, that we shall see these same, exact, above-mentioned truths even more strongly and consistently stated, strengthened, and supported.[48]

The next three occurrences of the word "cup" which we shall explore from within the sacred pages of the word of God, are found in 1 Corinthians, Chapter Ten, verses sixteen and twenty-one. Let us now examine them as they occur in their immediate and surrounding context.

> 1 Corinthians 10:14-21 states: "Therefore, my beloved, flee from idolatry. I speak as to wise men; judge for yourselves what I say. The cup of blessing which we bless, is it not the communion of the blood of Christ? The bread which we break, is it not the communion of the body of Christ? For we, *though* many, are one bread *and* one body; for we all partake of that one bread. Observe Israel after the flesh: Are not those who eat of the sacrifices partakers of the altar? What am I saying then? That an idol is anything, or what is offered to idols is anything? Rather, that the things which the Gentiles sacrifice they sacrifice to demons and not to God, and I do not want you to have fellowship with demons. You

---

[48] See Worksheet Summary on page 117.

cannot drink the cup of the Lord and the cup of demons; you cannot partake of the Lord's table and of the table of demons."

As any reader can easily probably already see, there are multiple problems encountered with any continued attempt or insistence on an absolutely literal rendering or interpretation of this passage in all aspects as well – including any attempt to insist on its demanding or mandating a lone, literal, single, physical communion cup to be used by Jesus' disciples… or else.

It should be just as equally obvious here as it has been on so many previous occasions that we have covered in this book, that the word "cup" in verse sixteen, continues to be used metaphorically or metonymically; as a figure of speech; as a symbol, summation, illustration, reference to, or representation of, what the actual, literal "cup" there actually contained - its contents, the fruit of the vine.

Just ask yourself, "Is 'The cup of blessing which we bless,' which is also referred to as the 'communion (fellowship or sharing) of the blood of Christ' in verse sixteen, insisting upon or referring exclusively or primarily to some lone, literal, physical cup? Or, is it not in far more likelihood, representing or referring to the blood-colored, blood-like substance or liquid – the "fruit of the vine" - which the "cup" contained or was 'of?'" Would it not be considered to be somewhat of a lack of common or biblical sense to understand that the answer to that question was anything other than the fruit of the vine which "the cup" contained, and that it was not referring specifically to the literal cup itself?

This is exactly the same thing as we saw from God's usage of the word "cup" in the gospel accounts when Jesus instituted the memorial designed to unify and make us one. The word "cup" there was also used to represent, symbolize, or to refer to the "fruit of the vine" which the cup contained; the "fruit of the vine" for which He gave thanks; the "fruit of the vine" which He told them to take and divide among themselves; the "fruit of the vine" which was the "it" they all drank of that made them one.

Additionally, if one were to continue to insist upon the singular word "cup" being taken as the absolutely literal representation of the New Covenant in His blood, instead of the word "cup" simply being used as a figure of speech to indicate the "fruit of the vine" it contained, then another related problem that would immediately arise as a result of such reasoning would be to seek to adequately answer the question, "Then what is the point of having any fruit of the vine in the cup at all?"

Think long and hard about this my beloved brethren. Don't just read over it without really turning this vital truth over in your minds a number of times. If the word "cup" here is the literal be all and end all; if the literal "cup" itself is our sharing in the blood of Christ; then why put any fruit of the vine in it at all? What's the point? After all, if the word "cup" is not being used as a metaphor, metonym, or to refer to or indicate its contents, then why put any "fruit of the vine" in it at all for communion?

If the word "cup" is not being used here to indicate its contents, then there's certainly no authority, at least in these verses, for any fruit of the vine ever being placed in "the cup" for the weekly celebrations of communion in Corinth. It's never mentioned. In fact, the phrase "fruit of the vine" never once occurs anywhere within either of the apostle Paul's divinely-dictated and inspired epistles to our first-century Corinthian brethren. Please also keep in mind that the church at that time did not have the complete, written, and revealed word of almighty God to go by as we do today.[49]

Don't miss this. If the Christians in the first-century congregation of the Lord's one, New Testament church in Corinth to whom Paul was writing did not yet have written copies of the gospels; and if they did NOT somehow understand at the same time that when the apostle Paul used the word "cup," that he was actually using it only as a vehicle to indicate or refer to its contents; then this teaching, taken absolutely and only literally, would mean that they all had to drink from an empty cup during communion – a teaching which would have surely both made no sense to them, and would have also had many of Paul's Corinthian brethren echoing Festus's sentiments about his being mad.[50]

---

[49] 1 Corinthians 13:8-11.
[50] Acts 26:24.

However, if instead, the word "cup" here in verse sixteen is being used by the apostle Paul in the same manner in which it was used by Jesus, that is to say, to refer to the "fruit of the vine" which it contained - and which is how, as we've seen, that we as God's children all over the world are told in Scripture we are to share our communion, or common union, under the New Covenant, and in the blood of Christ, with the Lord Jesus Christ as well as with one another when we drink of the fruit of the vine – then why all of the fuss, fighting, chaos, and division over the number of containers we as His disciples choose to use to do so?

Now, some who might be struggling to 'come to grips' (not literally, it's just another commonly used and easily and subconsciously processed figure of speech) with some of these scriptural truths which they've perhaps never before seen or been made aware of may proclaim, "But I just want to understand and obey Jesus!" And to that I say, "Amen! So, do I. So, let's do exactly that." Let us understand that when the Lord Jesus Christ commanded His disciples to take the cup and drink it in the gospels, that even though the cup was a literal, physical object, that He was referring to the "cup" in the same way that the Scriptures so often do: symbolically and to refer to its contents. The fruit of the vine from which all of His disciples are to drink and which makes them one as they do. Let us understand that this is the same Jesus who is recorded as telling His disciples in the gospel accounts to both take the cup and drink it, as well as to take the cup and divide it.

Hence, let us understand that when we put all of those texts together as we always must do in order to get the best possible understanding of any given biblical topic, that the only logical and common sense conclusion we can come to is that Jesus told His disciples to take the cup, divide its contents amongst themselves, and then drink the fruit of the vine – just as we do each and every Sunday in the Lord's church; and just as they also did in so many of the other congregations that that good sister and her family had to have driven right by on their way to Arkansas from Tulsa during their previously-mentioned trip to Oklahoma.

Look at verse sixteen again. Just as our sharing, fellowship, communion, or common union in the body of Christ is symbolized by the bread which we partake of in faithful obedience to His commandments, so too, is our sharing, fellowship, communion, or common union in the blood of Christ, symbolized by the fruit of the vine which we drink or partake of in faithful obedience to His commandments as well. Our common union in the body of Christ would not be shown by whether or not we all shared the same singular platter if one were mentioned as being under the bread to hold it, but would still be shown by whether or not we partook of the bread itself, would it not? It would. The platter would not have any importance or significance, other than as an implement necessary to the delivering of the bread. And the same is also true with "the cup."

Now again, at this point some may say, "But we're not talking about a platter or a tray that the bread may or may not possibly have been on, because the Scripture doesn't!" And they would be absolutely right. The Scripture doesn't have to mention whether or not a platter for the bread was there or not, because the bread didn't need one. A solid substance will set there by itself. It can be passed and distributed without something to stabilize it. However, a liquid substance cannot. It needs a "something" to contain it. Hence, the only reason for the mention of any "cup" whatsoever. Other than to stabilize and/or point out or refer to its contents, "the cup" or container itself has absolutely no other significance. This, just the same as "the cross" has/had no other significance than to stabilize and/or point out or refer to its divine Victim.

As we consider the apostle Paul's divinely-inspired instructions to his first-century Corinthian brethren, we also discover another major and additional problem, which pins the proponents of the 'one cup' perspective into an absolutely impossible and unsustainable theological position. First off, please recall the following excerpt from a personally-authored and previously posted article, placed back in Chapter Four:

> "But one of the saddest things associated with phone calls like that for me, lies in regards to what I consider to be one of the very simplest, most elementary, and most transparent and easy to see problems with the entire 'one cup'

perspective. This sister's home congregation on the east coast used one cup... while the Arkansas congregation with whom she and her family had worshipped previously – being one that also defends the 'one cup' doctrine as well - obviously used a different and additional cup from the one used at her home congregation on the east coast... as do all four of the congregations I supplied her with contact information for will use yet more and different, separate cups from either her home congregation, the one in Arkansas, or one another... just as will every other 'one cup' congregation in the world! Does anyone else besides me see the incredible irony and complete contradiction here?

The adherents to and defenders of the 'one cup' doctrine claim to be disciples and members of Jesus' one, biblical, faithful New Testament church worldwide. They claim to believe in and defend a doctrine of Jesus' disciples all drinking from the same one cup during communion... And yet, at the very same time that they defend a doctrine that ultimately divides the body of Christ, by dividing them from those who claim that Jesus' disciples can actually take communion from different cups, they themselves actually also use different and multiple communion cups from one another when they are in different congregations and locations! They have to! It is a physical impossibility for all of Jesus' disciples today all over the world to use 'one cup.' It simply cannot be done.

Thus, while they defend their 'one cup' doctrine to the point of actually dividing the body of Christ over it, severing and seeing themselves differently from those of their brethren who don't insist on their particular 'one cup' perspective, they themselves actually use more than one cup every Sunday (from hundreds of other 'one cup' disciples congregating in other locations)!

So which way is it? One cup, or multiple? One cup – absolutely no exceptions - as they insist upon during their doctrinal dissertations? Or one cup only when it is a matter of convenience - as they actually practice in reality? And how can they condemn the use of more than one communion cup amongst their brethren, when each and every single one of their 'one cup' congregations uses a different cup from each and every other one of their 'one cup' congregations, each and every single Sunday? In other words, when they themselves, while defending 'one cup,' actually use multiple cups?"

As just one example of some of the 'hoops' a person has to 'jump through' (another figure of speech of course, and not to be taken literally) in order to seek to justify a completely unjustifiable position due to its being 'built upon' a complete misunderstanding to begin with, a few years ago I had the privilege of pointing out some reasonable semblance of the above-mentioned article's sentiments to one rather convicted brother of the one cup persuasion.

His response was one which sought to try to find a way to justify their usage of multiple communion containers, while at the same time, aggressively insisting on the usage of only one. His reasoning process was as follows: That the Lord's Supper was modeled after the Passover. In their celebrating of the Passover, the people were commanded to use only one lamb per household. If the house was too small for the lamb, then they were to share it with their next door neighbor (Ex. 12:3-4). This, he said, was the symbolism that foreshadowed the usage of one cup per each congregation. (I must say I find it quite amazing that he sought to prove his perspective through the utilization of Old Testament symbolism, but yet continued to reject Jesus' very own usage of figurative or symbolic language when He referred to "this cup," which He then very clearly defined as "the fruit of the vine." Aren't we commanded by God to hear Jesus over Moses – Matthew 17:1-5? Yes.)

He then went on to point out that the Passover wasn't intended to be celebrated on a national level, but on a house by house level. Similarly, he said, the church doesn't worship, pray, sing, teach, give, or commune on a universal level either, but rather, on a congregation by congregation level. He therefore sought to conclude, that because each house had its own Passover lamb under the Old Covenant, and because our New Testament communion celebration 'is modeled after the Passover,' that each and every individual congregation as it worships independently today, can, does, and is able to have its own one cup, without violating or contradicting their whole 'one cup' insistence or perspective.

But, the insurmountable problem with this reasoning, the proverbial (not literal) 'fly in this ointment,' the incredible and colossal contradiction in his (*non*) comparison, is that each and every congregation of the Lord's one, New Testament church ever in existence, totally unlike and completely the exact opposite of every Jewish home in the Old Testament whose occupants celebrated the Passover, MUST SHARE THE SAME, ONE, LAMB, LORD, AND SAVIOR (Hebrews 10:1-14). Unlike and exactly the opposite of those Old Testament Passover celebrants, we, as New Testament congregations DO NOT each have our own, different, separate, sacrificial lamb.

Therefore, this reasoning, in reality, does not furnish any sort of support for the 'one cup' insistence, but quite to the contrary, supplies a resounding denunciation of it. And here's why... Just how do we all, in the thousands of congregations of the Lord's church in existence all over the world today, all share in the one, lone, same sacrificial Lamb's bloody and bodily sacrifice for each one of us, each and every Lord's Day, just as He commanded? Simple. By all partaking of the same two elements: the bread and fruit of the vine, which represent His body and blood, given to forgive us all.

This same truth is precisely what we discover when we once again re-visit the apostle Paul's divinely-dictated instructions to his Corinthian brethren in 1 Corinthians 10:16-17, which says:

> "The cup of blessing which we bless, is it not the communion of the blood of Christ? The bread which we break, is it not the communion of the body of Christ? For we, though many, are one

bread and one body; for we all partake of that one bread."

We need to understand that the apostle Paul, when he wrote this epistle to his Corinthian brethren, was at the time, located in, and writing from, the city of Ephesus (1 Cor. 16:8). This was about three hundred miles 'as the crow flies,' or an approximately eight day journey by sea at that time. And yet, what did he say? "The cup [singular] of blessing which we [we – both he, the brethren in Ephesus, as well as the brethren in Corinth; all of them, altogether] bless, is it not the communion of the blood of Christ?" Did you see it? If any person would continue to insist on the phrase "the cup," as meaning one, lone, literal, physical cup – and not being used metonymically to refer to its contents – then they are going to have to explain how the apostle Paul and his brethren in Ephesus, as well as all the brethren in Corinth some eight days of sea travel away, all managed to drink of that one, lone, literal, physical, singular cup each and every Lord's Day, and how they continually and consistently transported it back and forth so quickly. And what about all the other congregations in existence in those days? Did they not get to drink of "the cup?"

When I posed a similar query to the same aforementioned 'one-cup' brother, his response, in part, was: "Paul was actually referring to individuals within the [Ephesian] congregation [when he used the word "we"] and to the local congregation [of Ephesus and Corinth, when he used the word "body"]. At no time in this passage is the church universal under consideration."

So, in other words, his view was that when Paul wrote to the church at Corinth, he was telling the Corinthians that the cup of blessing which they in the Ephesian congregation ("we") blessed, and the bread which they in the Ephesian congregation broke, was communion of the local Ephesian congregation (body).' That makes no sense whatsoever - and on several scriptural as well as common sense levels.

To begin with, Paul in that passage is addressing the Corinthians and telling them what they need to know and do insofar as communion is concerned – not the Ephesian congregation (1 Corinthians 1:2). Hence, if Paul had been teaching that each congregation was to have its own, lone, singular communion cup in the manner in which this brother sought to portray, then in putting across his point of comparison between the two congregations to the Corinthians, Paul would have had to have said, "The cup of blessing which we bless, as well as the cup of blessing which you bless..." But he didn't say that did he? No. He indicated instead, that both the Ephesian as well as the Corinthian congregations, both drank of the same "cup."

Secondly, please notice that this brother gave no scriptural reference whatsoever in support of his stated opinion that, "At no time in this passage is the church universal under consideration." This, because just like with the so-called 'sinner's prayer of faith for salvation,' there isn't one. In fact, upon further consideration we find that just the opposite is true - and that we do have scriptural proof to back that up. Remember: the Bible is its own best interpreter. And the phrase "one body" as seen in verse seventeen (pointing back to the word "body" in verse sixteen), wherever it is used in reference to the spiritual body or church of Christ throughout the rest of Scripture, is ALWAYS used in reference to the one, entire, body or church[51], of Christ universally. We see this proven in places like 1 Corinthians 12:12-28, Ephesians 2:16, and especially of note, Ephesians 4:4-6. When Paul wrote in that passage that there was "one body, ...one Lord, one faith, one baptism, ...one God..." was he actually using the phrase "one body" to refer individually to each of the different congregations in different locations? No. If he had have been, then he would have used the word "bodies."

In the same context, this brother's reasoning would also have to mean that each, local, different, individual "body" or congregation, could legitimately therefore have its own local, different, individual Lord, faith, baptism, and God as well. Does that make any sense to anyone? No.

The fact is, that Paul was letting his Corinthian brethren know in no uncertain terms, that the entire, world-wide church of Christ membership, "though many, are one." And that whether from Ephesus where he was then, or Corinth to whom he was writing, and/or any and every other congregation

---

[51] 1 Corinthians 12:12-13; Ephesians 1:22-23; Colossians 1:18, 24.

anywhere in the world, were "one body" universally, and partakers of the 'one cup' and the "one bread" which made them all one.

The universal scope and coverage of this passage can also be easily seen and proven, simply by noting the context in which these two verses appear. From 1 Corinthians ten and verse one, right up through to and especially including verse eighteen, the entire, complete, and inarguable context is in regards to the one, national, overall and complete Old Testament people of God - Israel, in her entirety – and not anything whatsoever to do with different little pockets or groups thereof.

But, these are the sorts of Scripture-ravaging and context-defying hoops and loops one has to seek to create, 'jump through,' and 'drag others into' if they're going to continue to insist on a literal and physical understanding and application of metaphorical illustrations and metonymical representations. This, in the same manner as so many denominationalists have to do, in order to seek to justify their distortion and perversion of the message of the Book of Revelation.

And finally, if anyone ever needed even more numerous or powerful proofs positive that the word "cup" in this passage is being used metaphorically and not literally; that it is being used as a symbol, summation, illustration, or representation of something else and other than a literal drinking container, then here it is. Please re-read verse twenty-one. However literally the words "cup" and "table" are going to be taken in one occurrence in this verse, they must, of a necessity, be taken in the other. What is the "cup of demons" referring to here? What about the "table of demons?" Are the "cup" and "table" here talking about literal, physical elements? Did spirit beings such as demons set up to a literal table and drink from a lone and literal physical cup? Do demons even need such physical sustenance? If the word "cup" is only and always to be taken literally instead of figuratively, then these questions demand answers that make rock-solid sense.

Also, if one demands that these two terms, "cup" and "table," always be taken absolutely literally, then how does one "drink the cup?" They can't. You can't drink a solid, literal, physical cup. You can only drink its liquid contents. How does one literally partake of the Lord's literal table? They can't. You can't eat or partake of a solid, literal, physical wooden table.

Surely, the only common-sense conclusion that can be arrived at here, is exactly what the larger context these verses appear in and help to support so clearly reveals. This entire chapter is all about warning New Testament Christians not to follow faithless Israel's examples of disobedience by trying to follow the Lord only half-heartedly or part way, while at the same time indulging in evil, etc., as they had. Read verses one through twenty-two. It couldn't be clearer that that is the message of these verses. Nor could it be clearer that the word "cup" here, is primarily being used in a figurative or symbolic sense to refer to its contents, just as it so nearly always is in Scripture, could it? No.

The final five of the thirty-one total occurrences of the word "cup" in the New Testament, are also found in the apostle Paul's divinely-inspired instructions to the first-century congregation of the Lord's church in Corinth.

> 1 Corinthians 11:23-29 states: "For I received from the Lord that which I also delivered to you: that the Lord Jesus on the *same* night in which He was betrayed took bread; [24] and when He had given thanks, He broke *it* and said, 'Take, eat; this is My body which is broken for you; do this in remembrance of Me.' [25] In the same manner *He* also *took* the cup after supper, saying, 'This cup is the new covenant in My blood. This do, as often as you drink *it,* in remembrance of Me.' [26] For as often as you eat this bread and drink this cup, you proclaim the Lord's death till He comes. [27] Therefore whoever eats this bread or drinks *this* cup of the Lord in an unworthy manner will be guilty of the body and blood of the Lord. [28] But let a man examine himself, and so let him eat of the bread and drink of the cup. [29] For he who eats and drinks in an unworthy manner eats and drinks judgment to himself, not discerning the Lord's body.

It is simply impossible, after all we have thus far covered in this book regarding the Lord's constant and continual utilization of the term "cup" as a metaphorical or metonymical figure of speech, to signify, symbolize, represent, or refer to whatever the particular element or situation under consideration contained, to look at this passage and to not also realize that the word "cup" here is still being utilized the very same way by the Holy Spirit.

As we've repeatedly proven, just as the bread represents His body so too, it would be the fruit of the vine (and not the literal "cup" which simply contained it): for which He gave thanks; which represents His blood of the New Covenant; of which we partake as we drink; and which ultimately makes us spiritually one as we do so. All of this, just as Jesus intended, instructed, and clearly commanded.

And finally, as already discussed in a previous chapter, the phrase 'one cup' never once occurs in Scripture. For those who would still demand, defend, and insist on taking the word "cup" in an absolutely and exclusively lone, literal, singular, and physical fashion, they must understand that the actual and literal phrase in Scripture which they must now therefore defend and insist upon, is not just about using a cup, 'one cup,' any cup, or "the cup," but only the one, lone, literal, actual, "***this*** cup," which the Lord Jesus used, and which phrase the apostle Paul also cited in this text (Luke 22:20; 1 Corinthians 11:25, 26, and 27). You say, "But, that's impossible," and you're right. But such is the impossible and unsustainable 'corner' and position one inevitably 'paints themselves into,' whenever they seek to understand, apply, and insist upon implementing the Lord's figures of speech in a literal and/or physical fashion. Just ask Nicodemus; or the disciples who stayed with Jesus in John Chapter Six; or better yet, the disciples who walked away from and followed Him no more in that same chapter when they thought He might be instituting some form of cannibalism.

Our Lord Jesus Christ constantly used figures of speech (Jn. 16:25, 29). One of His most oft-utilized teaching tools was the metaphor – using a common item or object to symbolize, represent, apply, or refer to something other than itself (just as He did with the "cross" in Mk. 8:34, Lk. 9:23, and Matt. 10:38). Remember, the Bible is its own best interpreter; and between God, Jesus, and the Holy Spirit, the word "cup" is used 31 times, in 28 verses, of the NKJV translation of the New Testament, and in every one of them it is used metaphorically, as the chart below clearly illustrates.

Text & Number of Times The Word "Cup" Occurs:	What the word "cup" was actually, metaphorically used to symbolize, represent, apply or refer to...
Matthew 10:42; (2): Mark 9:41	Even the smallest of blessings...
Matthew 20:22-23; (4): Mark 10:38-39	The suffering encountered/contained in a life devoted to following God...
Matthew 23:25-26; (3): Luke 11:39	The Pharisees' spiritual condition...
Matthew 26:27; (11): Mark 14:23; Luke 22:17-20; 1 Corinthians 10:16, 11:25-28	The fruit of the vine contained in the cup, which symbolizes our common oneness and sharing in the shed blood of Jesus Christ under the New Covenant.
Matthew 26:39, 42; (5): Mark 14:36; Luke 22:42; John 18:11	The entire scope of suffering contained in the crucifixion. (He wasn't talking about an actual, literal "cup" in these texts!)
1 Corinthians 10:21 (2):	The consequences contained in the lifestyle choices we make, regarding whom we follow and how we live.
Revelation 14:10, (2): 16:19	The full and undiluted scope and contents of God's wrath and indignation...
Revelation 17:4, (2): 18:6	The full, undiluted scope of the "great harlot's," or "Babylon's" sins.

NOTES

Chapter Ten:

The Chronicle

In the previously-referenced, June 22, 2016 article revealing the results of an interview with one of the more well-known and widely recognized preachers and proponents of the 'one cup' perspective, there were several comments, components, comparisons, and considerations which I would, at this point, be extremely remiss if I did not scripturally address. But please keep in mind as we continue, that I do not personally know, nor do I believe that I have ever met this brother whose words and doctrine we shall now address. The following is nothing more or less than an honest, objective, and sincere biblical examination of his words, just as, and in the same way in which I hope people will seriously, sincerely, objectively, and most importantly, scripturally, examine the words and doctrines put forward in this book, before ever accepting, adopting, or implementing any of them.

The written article resulting from the interview was entitled, "No Such Thing As Individual Communion."[52] This is a title, the wording of which in my humble opinion, is, at its very best, more than just a little bit misleading to begin with. After all, no one I know of is even remotely suggesting, advocating, seeking to support, or promoting anything akin to 'individual communion[53],' but simply proving that to partake of the fruit of the vine together, after having first divided it down amongst ourselves just as the first-century disciples who had gathered together that night with Jesus most surely must have done in compliance with His commandments (as recorded in Luke 22:17-20) is certainly not

---

[52] "No Such Thing As Individual Communion," Christian Chronicle, Lynn McMillon, June 22, 2016, http://www.christianchronicle.org/article/no-such-thing-as-individual-communion.
[53] 1 Corinthians 12:20-25.

sinful; nor is it anywhere close to being as condemnation-incurring as to implement and insist on binding certain rules or laws which God never bound – and especially to the point of dividing Christ's blood-bought church down over such, and then summarily condemning all of those who do not share or support that particular perspective on the issue. However, and unfortunately, as we shall soon discover, the deceptive nature of the title's wording can also be seen to permeate, penetrate, and resonate throughout entire sections of this less than aptly or accurately entitled article.

One of the first things that this 'one cup' brother was asked to do, was to please explain the reasons for using only one cup in the Lord's Supper. According to the published article, his response was that those of his particular perspective used only one cup during the Lord's Supper for the following five reasons:

- *"To preserve this divine ordinance "just as it was delivered," as we read in 1 Corinthians 11:2."*

If only that were true according to the Scriptures… but alas, and sadly, it isn't. But please don't take my word for it. And please don't take his, theirs, or anyone else's other than God's for it either. Instead, check it out for yourself in the Scriptures. The apostle Paul, in penning the passage cited in the above response, had "just… delivered" some divinely-inspired instructions about "the cup" in the immediately-preceding chapter - Chapter Ten of 1 Corinthians. In that chapter (just as we also covered at length in the immediately-preceding chapter of this book, Chapter Nine) the apostle Paul unmistakably and inarguably indicated that "the cup of blessing" [singular], was something shared by both himself, the Ephesian congregation from whence he was writing, and also the Corinthian congregation to whom he was writing, which were some three hundred miles, or approximately eight days' travel time apart. In fact, he further indicated (through his usage of the term "one body" in verse seventeen), that the one, entire, universal body or church of Christ, all partook of the same one bread, and "cup." There is just no possible way that he was therefore referring to any one, lone, literal, physical loaf or cup to be used by all Christians, but that he was simply using the term "the cup" metonymically, to indicate or refer to its contents - the fruit of the vine.

Otherwise, and if such is not the case, then perhaps our denominational friends and neighbors who only celebrate communion once a year instead of once a week have a point. After all, it might have taken a year to get that 'one cup' circulated to every first century congregation of the Lord's church in those days.

Additionally, if the wording in this phrase is to be taken as absolutely literally as our 'one cup' brethren would so vigorously contend, instead of figuratively as we've so often seen done by God in the Scriptures, then the literal cup would obviously be full of literal, physical, tangible "blessing." How does that work exactly?

And so we see, that contrary to this interviewed brother's answer, that to truly "preserve this divine ordinance '*just as it was delivered*,'" one would only have to come together or assemble with their brethren in any given location or congregation (such as Ephesus, Corinth, Tulsa, or London), break the bread and divide the fruit of the vine, and then consume them just as their blood-bought brethren all over the world would also be doing each Lord's Day as well, just as we have previously covered. That's what truly preserving this divine ordinance "just as it was delivered" is comprised of - according to Scripture.

- The second response: "*Because the scriptural precedent for how to observe the Lord's Supper — with one loaf and one cup — is as weighty as for when to observe it (on "the first day of the week," as we read in Acts 20:7). The Scriptures regarding how to partake of the Lord's Supper are even more emphatic ("do this"), including Mark 14:23, Luke 22:19 and 1 Corinthians 11:24-25.*"

Let's examine this two-sentence response, in two separate parts. In other words, we're going to 'divide it' down before seeking to disseminate and 'drink it in.'

I believe that this first sentence is absolutely and completely scripturally correct – with the glaring exception of the blatant insertion and expression of the scripturally-unproven, personally-held opinion that was so seemingly-assertively stuck in between the hyphens.[54] Jesus commanded His gathered disciples that night, to "Take this (the fruit of the vine as metonymically referred to by the phrase 'the cup' in the preceding sentence) and divide it among [them]selves" (Luke 22:17). If ever there was a verse in Scripture – and there are many when examined in their original, biblical, and consistent context just as we've studied throughout this book - that cast some very serious aspersions on the whole 'one cup or else' insistence, this is it. Does anyone seriously believe that the disciples divided *it* (the fruit of the vine as metonymically referred to by the phrase "the cup" in the preceding sentence) among themselves by pouring it into their hand, or anything else, other than into their own, separate, individual, cups or containers before drinking *it* as commanded by Jesus at the table that night?

The second sentence of the above-reported response is also quite correct insofar as its emphasis on the manner in which one is to partake of the Lord's Supper being vitally important in Scripture. But; what is so ironically noteworthy as well in that sentence, is that while on the one hand the respondent realizes and recognizes the emphatic nature of the term "do this;" and while he equally and absolutely insists on an absolutely literal usage of the word "cup" (singular, literal, and physical); he is

---

[54] Just as an interesting point of comparison for the reader's consideration: In 2 Peter 2:1, Peter warned of those who would "secretly bring in destructive heresies." In brother Guy N. Wood's commentary on 2 Peter (Guy N. Woods, *Gospel Advocate Company*, (1983) 163.), he says that the word 'privily' (translated 'secretly' in the New King James Version as quoted herein), means, "to slip in by the side of, and indicates that these teachers had artfully and slyly introduced their false doctrines by the side of the truth in such a fashion as to deceive those who had accepted them." Now, that does not mean that this is the case in every situation – nor even the majority of them - wherein a conclusion is stated alongside, or as a summation of, a biblical truth. Oft times (hopefully) such a conclusion or summation is stunningly correct; at other times it may be somewhat incorrect, although certainly and sincerely not through any intentional effort whatsoever to be misleading; and then there are those situations such as brother Woods described. It is always up to the individual seeker to search the Scriptures daily, test the spirits fully, and then decide which of these is the case and what they can therefore best stand before God with (Acts 17:11; 1 John 4:1-6; Romans 14:12-13).

never once quoted as emphasizing or insisting on an absolutely literal or emphatic insistence on the actual, literal, biblical phraseology which perfectly places and utilizes both of those two terms together. However, would that not be the next logical step? And yet, while the heavily defended phrase 'one cup' never actually occurs in Scripture anywhere, the phrase which utilizes both the words "this" and "cup" does... in fact, eight different times!

The actual phrase, "this cup," occurs four times in Scripture (metonymically of course as we've so thoroughly discussed) to indicate, point to, or refer to the sufferings which would be contained in the Christ's crucifixion experience (Matthew 26:39, 42; Mark 14:36; and Luke 22:42). And that same phrase, "this cup," also occurs another four times (again, metonymically of course as we've so thoroughly discussed) to indicate, point to, or refer to the fruit of the vine which the "this cup" Jesus held in His hand contained (Luke 22:20; 1 Corinthians 11:25, 26, and 27).

However, if one is going to demand an absolutely literal interpretation and insistence on every such word – even when Jesus has been repeatedly proven to have been constantly and continually utilizing some of them in common, everyday, figureative language to indicate something else and other than themselves – then in the name of consistency[55], one has to also demand nothing less than an absolutely and aggressively all-out insistence on using the same, one, lone, literal "*this* cup," as was actually stated in Scripture four different times in reference to communion. Why do they not do ***this***? Perhaps because the usage of that one, lone, literal, particular, physical "*this* cup" which Jesus used is obviously impossible today, and therefore puts the promoter and supporter of such a perspective into a totally unsustainable scriptural position? That would be my guess. But, that's the inevitable 'corner' one usually, eventually, and inevitably 'paints' themselves into, if and when they fail to understand the difference between literal and figurative language usage.

---

[55] Romans 2:17-24.

- The third response to the previously-posed question: *"Because Jesus' instructions on how to 'divide' (share) the cup in Luke 22:17 authorize only one cup. 'Drink from it, all of you,' He says in Matthew 26:27."*

Once again, just as with the wording of this article's title, the wording used in the first sentence of this response is also "at its very best, more than just a little bit misleading." To begin with, Jesus' instructions on how to "divide" the cup in Luke 22:17 DO NOT DO ANYTHING AKIN TO authorizing only one cup – even when taken together with Matthew 26:27 just as we already explored, examined, and discussed at great length and in intricate detail in Chapter Eight.

And secondly, although there are several similarities in the two terms placed side by side in that initial sentence (i.e., "divide" and "share"), there are also definite and definitive differences between the meanings, nuances, and understandings conveyed by the 'dividing' of something, as opposed to the just simply 'sharing' of it. For example, several Christians may "share" a pew on Sunday morning, but it creates a quite different picture in another's mind to report later that they had "divided" the pew.

The scriptural difference between these two terms is also extremely obvious when one examines the definition of the Greek word which Luke used by divine inspiration in that particular passage as well. According to Vine's[56], the Greek word which God led Luke[57] to use in that verse which we translate as "divide," is the compound word *"diamerizo,"* the definition of which Vine's says is: "completely, to divide up." It is formed by the combining of two Greek words, *"dia"* (meaning "through"), and *"merizo"* (meaning "to divide through"). Now, although Vine's makes mention in its definition of this second word, *"merizo,"* that it: "in the middle voice means 'to divide anything with another, to share with,'" Vine's also makes it very clear that the **primary** meaning of *"merizo"* is, "a part, to part, divide into," and that "the usual

---

[56] *Vine's Expository Dictionary of Biblical Words* (Nashville: Thomas Nelson, Inc, Publishers, 1986) 178.
[57] See 2 Timothy 3:16-17, and 2 Peter 1:20-21.

meaning is 'to divide.'" Now, keeping in mind the usual and primary meaning of the word *"merizo"* as discussed; and keeping in mind that *"merizo"* is only the second part of the actual compound word which Luke used there in that verse; and keeping in mind Vine's actual definition of the actual Greek word *"diamerizo"* which Luke did utilize there; it would seem to me at least (as well as the translators obviously), to be quite a stretch indeed to seek to convey that Jesus was telling His disciples to simply "share," instead of to "divide," "the cup." But of course, any continued insistence that Jesus was referring to "the cup" in an exclusively literal fashion (instead of figuratively, referring to its fruit of the vine contents) when He told His disciples to "divide *it*," requires precisely that sort of 'stretch' as 'par for the course,' in order to justify and make such misunderstandings of figurative language 'a little easier to swallow' as it were.

- The fourth response to the previously-posed question: ***"Because the cup containing the fruit of the vine has spiritual significance, as we read in Luke 22:20 and 1 Corinthians 11:25."***

With all due respect, and hopefully with the same sort of love and spirit Jesus had as He confronted a less than accurate doctrine of a deeply religious group in His day[58], no it doesn't. Let the reader go back and very carefully re-read both of those verses in his/her own personal Bible. In neither one of those passages does "the cup" have any spiritual significance whatsoever. This is because, as we have so completely, extensively, exhaustively, and perhaps even a little bit redundantly covered throughout so much of the immediately-preceding chapters of this book, when Jesus either referred to or used the word "cup," His continual and habitual pattern was to do so metaphorically or metonymically; as a figure of speech to indicate the contents contained within the element or situation under consideration. Therefore, the only significance of the "cup" in these verses, is as a necessary container for its all-important liquid contents; its liquid contents which **do** have

---

[58] Matthew 22:29.

spiritual significance; its liquid contents **for** which Jesus gave thanks; and its liquid contents **from** which He told His disciples to drink: the fruit of the vine which symbolizes or represents His blood of the New Covenant; the fruit of the vine which makes us all one under that blessed and blood-instituted covenant; and the fruit of the vine which we all come together and assemble to obediently partake of after dividing it down among ourselves "in remembrance of [Him]," just as He instructed His closest disciples to do that night, and just as His faithful church has done ever since (Luke 22:19-20).

But before moving on, it is once again incredibly interesting to note that although both of the verses cited in this response contain the phrase "this cup," that those of the exclusively literal-insistent nature when it comes to the "cup," go absolutely nowhere near as aggressively insisting on using that, one, lone, literal, physical, exact, "_**this**_ cup," that is clearly and literally mentioned in both of the verses cited in the above response. Why is that? Perhaps because it is obviously physically impossible to find, verify, and/or use *it* universally… sort of like it is for all of Jesus' hundreds of thousands of disciples today, to all drink from the same, one, lone, literal, container, but yet very easy for them all to drink of the fruit of the vine wherever on the planet they may find themselves assembled to commune together.

- The fifth and final response to the previously-posed question: ***"To safeguard the sharing, joint participation and intimacy inherent in the word 'communion' (1 Corinthians 10:16). The phrase 'individual communion' is a contradiction."***

If really and sincerely safeguarding "the sharing, joint participation, and intimacy inherent in the word 'communion'" as evidenced in 1 Corinthians 10:16, is truly that all-important to our brethren of the 'one cup' persuasion and perspective, then may I take just a moment to 'bare my heart,' and to beg, plead, beseech, and to humbly appeal to each and every one of my beloved 'one cup' brethren in Christ who might ever read or be made aware of the contents of this book, to please,

PLEASE then, biblically 'pour over,' re-read, research, and prayerfully[59] reconsider everything I've stated in this book from your very own Bibles? And then, to truly take to heart and mind the very sound and contextual teaching found in both the verse cited above, as well as the one that immediately follows it (1 Corinthians 10:16-17): That the apostle Paul, as well as his beloved brethren in Ephesus *from where* he was writing, plus all of his beloved brethren in Corinth *to whom* He was writing (some several hundred miles and more than a week's travel away in those days), all had the opportunity to enjoy that same spiritual oneness, "sharing, joint participation, and [spiritual] intimacy inherent in the word communion," as they assembled and gathered together in their separate locations and congregations each and every Lord's Day (along with the rest of the Lord's one church or one body wherever they were in the world), and broke and partook of the bread, and divided and drank of the fruit of the vine – referred to metonymically as "the cup of blessing" - which the apostle Paul said they all blessed. This is what made them all spiritually one then; it is what makes us all spiritually one today; and it is what will make all of Jesus' disciples spiritually one until the day He comes to take His faithful church home.

But the respondent was right about one thing. And that was when he stated that *"The phrase 'individual communion' is a contradiction."* It is. That's why after the prayer of blessing is said for the fruit of the vine here each Lord's Day, that we do just as so many thousands of other faithful congregations of the Lord's people the world over do; we distribute and drink the fruit of the vine together, in the minute or two before the next element of worship commences.

In the next portion of the interview, this same 'one cup' insistent brother was asked about the health risk involved in using just one communion cup per congregation. In the midst of citing several secular sources in an attempt to promote the particular viewpoint that the health risks associated with the usage of but one communion cup per congregation need not be a concern, he stated that, *"We do not consider health risk a*

---

[59] James 1:5-6.

relevant problem in obeying Jesus' command for the assembled to share the cup" - yet another prime example of a "more than just a little bit misleading to begin with" statement. This, because just as we've repeatedly seen, Jesus never commanded nor intended for His assembled disciples to divide and share the literal cup, but to divide and share its contents - the fruit of the vine. And besides, even if He had been using the term "cup" literally instead of figuratively - which He wasn't as we've seen, but if He had have been as our 'one-cup' insistent brethren so tenaciously seem to want to proclaim – then it is significant to notice that it wasn't literally just 'a cup,' 'any cup,' 'some cup,' or even 'one cup' that He commanded, but only that one, lone, literal, particular "***this*** cup" which Jesus Christ held in His very own, soon to be bound, pierced, and bloodied hand that night. It was indeed "***this cup***" which was the literal phrase that our Savior was cited eight different times in the gospel accounts as having spoken, as previously noted and cited.

However, another troubling aspect of the response to the question regarding health risk (in addition to the total lack of understanding regarding the difference between when God's word is using figurative as opposed to literal language), was the attempt to try to tie, imply, infer, or convey the idea to today's Christian, that 'multiple communion containers' was originally a doctrine of the denominational world and therefore a departure from New Testament teaching; and that we must therefore, automatically not adopt or follow it if we would be faithful to Jesus. Nor was this attempt limited to just his initial response, which was:

- *"This is an important question because it is the reason denominational leaders initiated the individual communion service in the 1890's — and why some Churches of Christ followed their lead about 20 years later..."*

If the concept or implication intended by this statement is what I suspect – that what our 'one-cup' brethren perceive or understand to be the practice or 'innovation' of using multiple communion containers as having originated in the denominations due to a result of health concerns - and that their usage is therefore 'off-limits' to true New Testament Christians – then they'd better get rid of their church buildings. They simply have no New Testament authority for them. New Testament Christians met in the temple, private homes[60] (very presumably with kitchen facilities by the way), schools[61], and many other places, but we never see them meeting in, nor do we ever see the literal term 'church building(s)' in the Scriptures. Research in fact, concludes that 'church buildings' were first built and utilized by the apostate Roman Catholic Church[62]... 'and most churches of Christ followed their lead many years later' – including of course, the vast majority of our 'one cup' brethren.

Speaking of this idea of church buildings and not wanting to do anything whatsoever that our denominational friends and neighbors do just simply because they do it, one good brother who reviewed this manuscript prior to its publication quipped to me that he had heard brother Wendell Winkler make a comment along the line that, since Baptists go in through the front door, we had better go in through the windows because we don't want to be denominational. Doesn't sound to me like too much of a 'leap' at all from the point that this 'one cup' brother was apparently trying to 'push through' to us.

And then, there is the idea of websites. Seeing as how we do not see the literal term 'website' anywhere in the Scriptures, unless it is absolutely provable that the very first religious organization ever to have a website was a congregation of the Lord's church, then by the same exact implication as seemingly intended above (that is, that any idea or concept originating in any denomination, is always, absolutely, and automatically wrong, with absolutely no exceptions whatsoever), our one cup brethren had better get rid of not only their buildings, but their websites and every other so-called 'innovation' not seen literally in evidence in the Scriptures. This, or else be viewed as

---

[60] Acts 5:42.
[61] Acts 19:9.
[62] "Why and when did Christians start constructing special buildings for worship?" Christianity Today, Everett Ferguson, accessed June 23, 2018, https://www.christianitytoday.com/history/2008/november/why-and-when-did-christians-start-constructing-special.html.

inconsistent at best, and/or hypocritical at worst. After all, the Lord literally said to "Go… and preach."[63] When they post and send out religious information on a website, they don't literally 'go,' even though *it* – the gospel - does. So which way is it brethren?

Now, this is not to say that the practice of using multiple communion cups did actually originate in the denominational world. After all, the absolutely necessary inference inherent in Jesus' command in Luke 22:17 to His disciples to "Take this [the cup containing the fruit of the vine] and divide *it* among [them]selves" unquestionably demands that they all had their own cup to divide *it* into before drinking *it*.

Nonetheless, this brother continued to 'beat the drum' for a less than biblical origin of the usage of multiple communion cups, despite the 'contents' of Luke 22:17-20. Some of his later statements 'along that line' included the following:

- "As the 19th century Christian scholar J. W. McGarvey said, 'If it is wrong to change in the slightest degree the ordinance of baptism, it is still worse, if possible, to change the ordinance of the Lord's Supper.' …McGarvey also pressed these points in his column in the ***Christian Standard*** on June 25, 1904: *Whatever may be the special pleading in excuse for this innovation, it is perfectly clear that it aims to avoid that which the Lord enjoined in instituting the Supper; that is, the use of the same cup by a number of individuals. He could have directed each of the twelve to drink from his own cup, had he adjudged that to be the better way. But he did not, and we shall be far more likely to please him by doing what he did than by doing what he avoided.*

With all due respect to brother McGarvey, while his first statement as posted above is completely and inarguably correct (that it is wrong to change in the slightest, either the ordinance of baptism or the Lord's Supper), his next few statements have been repeatedly, scripturally, and consistently shown to be far

---

[63] Mark 16:15.

less than accurate throughout this study. No, it is nowhere near "perfectly clear" that multiple communion cups in any way negates or avoids what the Lord enjoined in instituting the supper. In fact, as we have so thoroughly and repeatedly proven, Luke 22:17-20 demands that we understand that each disciple had to have had his own cup that night, into which he poured his own share of the fruit of the vine which Jesus commanded them to divide among themselves; that they did not, as a number of individuals, all use the same cup, but that they instead, divided its contents down amongst themselves just as Jesus commanded; and that Jesus did thereby, in effect, adjudge that each of the twelve drink from his own cup. Or, said another way (if I may utilize brother McGarvey's words - only in a bit more biblically-accurate fashion in this instance): "He (the Lord) could have directed each of the twelve to drink from His (the Lord's) own cup, had He adjudged that to be the better way. But He (the Lord) did not, instead commanding them to divide the contents (the fruit of the vine) of His cup down among themselves (as Luke recorded) and then to drink that divided down fruit of the vine (just as Matthew and Mark recorded)." This makes perfect sense. And the reason why is because it perfectly combines and harmonizes all of the gospel accounts of this event.

However, the latter portion of brother McGarvey's last sentence as quoted above is quite correct. We shall indeed, be far more likely to please Jesus by doing what He did, than by doing what He avoided. And what He did, was to have them divide it, before they drank it.

Another statement furnished in response, presumably to additionally try to tie, imply, infer, or convey the idea to today's Christian that 'multiple communion containers' was originally a doctrine of the denominational world and/or a departure from New Testament teaching, was:

- "Men forced needless division upon the church with this burgeoning denominational trend. G.C. Brewer wrote in his 1948 autobiography: *'I think I was the first preacher to advocate the use of the individual communion cup,*

> *and the first church in the State of Tennessee that adopted it was the church for which I was preaching, the Central Church of Christ at Chattanooga, Tennessee, then meeting in the Masonic Temple. My next work was with the church at Columbia, Tennessee, and, after a long struggle, I got the individual communion service into that congregation. ... Of course, I was fought both privately and publicly.'* Any change in a teaching that was practiced for almost 20 centuries after the time of Jesus is at the least questionable and at the most unacceptable. The use of the common drinking vessel was so entrenched that brother Brewer had to battle within the body to promote the novel practice."

It is entirely possible that in the days both during, and immediately following the Restoration Movement's humble and pioneering beginnings on American soil, that many congregations may indeed have used only one cup. It may have been wooden, glass, ceramic, or some other substance. It may have been used, in some cases, out of either convenience, human insistence, biblical ignorance, or for some other less-apparent reason. But remember: As we shall discuss more in-depth in our next chapter, the problem here is **NOT** whether a congregation uses one, or multiple communion containers. That is NOT the issue. The problem here, is when men 'force needless division upon the church,' by insisting on making and binding certain rules or laws on their beloved and blood-bought brethren which God did not; and additionally insisting that their way is the ONLY WAY... or else. Both the Lord's Old Testament people, as well as His one, New Testament church have both been 'down this road' before (Matthew 23:16-24; Acts 15:1).

Okay, so brother Brewer had a difficult time changing the 'status quo' in the congregations where he served. Probably every gospel preacher who has ever sought to introduce any new, but still biblically-acceptable challenge, plan, program, process, or procedure into the congregation where he served has encountered exactly the same battle. How many song leaders have encountered those saints so entrenched in the "Announcements, two songs, opening prayer, two songs, communion, one song, sermon, invitation song, closing prayer, and then closing song order of service," that should they alter or deviate from it even the least little fraction, that they get an awful 'earful' on the way out, from the "But, that's not the way we've always done it" crowd? How much resistance did some preachers and teachers get for switching from chalk and flannel boards to PowerPoint presentations? People get into a rut, get comfortable, and don't want to be challenged to change or get out of it – even if it is an entirely and completely biblically-sound and acceptable concept.

And finally, if I may reconstitute the second to the last sentence of the above quoted and reported response: **"Any change in a teaching that was instituted and practiced almost 20 centuries ago by none other than Jesus Himself is completely unacceptable.** That is precisely the purpose of this book: To help every single saint alive today to understand that faithfully obeying Jesus' nearly twenty-centuries old instruction to take, to divide amongst ourselves, and then to drink the fruit of the vine which makes us all one as we do, just as His first-century church all over the world did on the first day of each week, certainly cannot be wrong or sinful!

NOTES

Chapter Eleven:

The Conclusions

Before coming to the actual concluding thoughts and portion of this book, we must examine a few of the remaining responses made, prior to the conclusion of the interview which we began examining in Chapter Ten.

When asked if there were other differences between individual and multiple cup congregations of the churches of Christ, the response, in part, was:

- *"Many [multi-cup] congregations have women teachers in publicly advertised Bible classes. This practice is rooted in denominationalism, not Scripture (1 Timothy 2:11-15, 1 Corinthians 14:34-35). ...The Scriptures are very explicit: 'Let your women keep silent in the churches ('in the assemblies,' as Young's Literal Translation reads), for they are not permitted to speak' (1 Corinthians 14:34).*

    We find no biblical authority for segregated Bible classes. When the early church assembled, they 'came together into one place' (1 Corinthians 11:17-20, 33-34, 14:23-26). ...Even friends of the segregated assembly now question the practical argument they once presented in its favor."

FTD: "Failure To Differentiate." If ever there was a common theme or thread that seemed to run through so much of the 'heart and soul' of the sentiments expressed in the aforementioned article, as well as having to be thoroughly addressed at length in this book, "Failure To Differentiate" would seem to constitute one of the primary ones. And here we see that same "FTD" raise its caustic, chaotic, and confusion-inducing head once again. The specific sentiments expressed in the first and bulleted paragraph above, regarding the context, contents, and commandments contained in 1 Corinthians 14 (insofar as women needing to remain silent in our assemblies) are correct. However, the "failure to differentiate" between what that chapter is specifically addressing, and other times, such as when women are teaching other women as Scripture commands them to[64], forces yet another, exclusive, 'one size fits all,' 'this way or else' perspective just as we see in evidence in the above response. Please permit me to explain via a few slightly-edited excerpts, from a previously, personally authored study…

> It quickly becomes obvious to anyone, from the most casual reader to the most intense student of the Word of God as they contemplate the contents and context of First Corinthians, Chapter Fourteen, that it was written specifically in reference to the worship assembly; the worship assembly wherein the saints all gather together to commune, and give, etc., on the Lord's Day. Verses 5, 12, 19, and 23-35 (which see), all make this abundantly clear, as does the fact that in the original Greek, the phrase used is *"en ekklesia,"* or, "in the assembly." First Corinthians, Chapter Fourteen, is all about *the* worship assembly, wherein they specifically came together (1 Corinthians 14:23, 26; see also Chapter 11:17, 18, 20, 33, and 34); all together as a church, for: singing, praying, worshipping, communing, giving, and learning and being encouraged from the revered and revealed Will of God. Scriptural context clearly bears this out, as this is in a section of Scripture wholly devoted to giving instructions on the activities within the Sunday "worship assembly." We see this exclusive "worship assembly" context clearly began in Chapter

---

[64] Titus 2:2-5.

Eleven with the apostle Paul's discussion of the elements of the Lord's Supper, and then concluded in Chapter Sixteen with their first day of the week in the assembly instructions on giving.

In *that* assembly, the women are to remain "silent" (Gk. *"sigao"*; "without sound"), with the exception of congregational singing which all the saints in the congregations are to do (Ephesians 1:1, 5:19, Colossians. 1:2, 3:16, etc.). The '*sigao* silence' in *the* assembly was for all churches of Christ for all time and in every place (verse 33), and was and is, a "command of the Lord" (verse 37).

However, there are several and distinct differences between the exclusive, "in the [worship] assembly" context there, and the "everywhere" else context of 1 Timothy 2:8-15, which is also cited in the above response. While God Himself prohibits Christian women from teaching or having authority (leading) over Christian men "everywhere" (1 Timothy 2:8), conversely, women of God do have some teaching responsibilities to carry out which they are specifically expected by God Himself to do (as outlined in Titus 2:3-5; a chapter in which Paul later tells Timothy to: "Declare these things; exhort and rebuke with all authority. Let no one despise you"), and, as some see reflected in 2 Timothy 1:5; namely, that Christian women are specifically expected by God, to teach younger Christian women, as well as to help with teaching the children (even though the final responsibility for children's teaching 'rests' on their father's 'shoulders' - Ephesians 6:1-4).

The problem in the above response, is a total and complete "Failure To Differentiate" between the Lord's Day worship assembly (wherein we all come together as a church to sing, pray, worship, commune, give of our means, and learn from the preached, revered, and revealed Will of God), and every time other than that. When members of faithful 'multi-cup' congregations assemble or "come together in one place" as a church, specifically for the express purpose of the aforementioned worship assembly, and to therefore experience the aforementioned worship elements, we are not, and do not, segregate, nor separate, in any way, shape, or form. However, an hour or so prior to and before the beginning of that worship assembly, many 'multi-cup' congregations make the most of the time (Ephesians 5:15-17) by studying the Bible together in smaller, age and knowledge appropriate groups (or classes). In faithful congregations, women neither teach nor have authority over men as leaders of any of those adult Bible classes (1 Timothy 2:12-13), but they certainly do teach some of the children's classes - something that a "Failure To Differentiate" between when the Bible is specifically addressing the worship assembly, as opposed to all other times, would obviously prevent as seen in the above response. But, who would have ever have thought it? A group of Christians who are anti-**Bible study**?!? Maybe that might help to explain, at least in part, any such lack of knowledge as could cause some to be confused over when Jesus was using a figure of speech, as opposed to literal language...?

And then came the clincher; in one, final, flawed, feeble, frail, and ill-fated attempt to somehow seek to justify the determined and divisive lack of fellowship with their also blood-bought brethren in so many 'multiple cup' congregations, when asked if 'one-cup' congregations considered themselves to be in fellowship with other churches of Christ, this was the response:

- *"We see this departure from the New Testament in the same light as many multi-cup congregations view those who have introduced instrumental music into their worship services and so do not consider them to be in fellowship with us."*

Then may I very humbly, very meekly, and very lovingly perhaps suggest, that like our brethren in the first century congregation of the city of Laodicea were commanded to do by Jesus, that those who hold such views might please, _**please**_ consider "anoint[ing their] eyes with eye salve, that [they] may see? (Revelation 3:18)" – not literally, but figuratively speaking, just as Jesus was yet once again doing of course. Because as we have seen and discussed again, …and again, …and again, …and again, …and again, throughout so much of this study, dividing down the fruit of the vine before drinking it just as Jesus commanded His first-century disciples to do, is certainly no departure from, but a faithful following of, New Testament doctrine.

May I also very lovingly but firmly 'note' that the comparison about seeing us in the 'same light' (Did you notice how the respondent there – who has failed to this point to recognize the difference between literal and figurative language when it comes to Jesus' reference to the "cup" - used a figure of speech there himself in seeking to make his point? Incredible!) as we "view those who have introduced instrumental music into their worship services" also proves the need for such 'eye salve' as well, and here's why. If the word "play" was as inherent in or indicated by the word "sing," as the "fruit of the vine" is obviously indicated by the word "cup" in the Scriptures, then it would make sense. Or, if the Scriptures said of Jesus: "Then He sang the song, and gave thanks, and said, 'Learn this and play it among yourselves; for I say to you, I will not play this song again until the kingdom of God comes.' …Likewise He also took the lute after supper, saying, 'This lute is the New Covenant in my blood,'" then I could understand his comparison.

Yes; if Jesus had, by His example, inferred or authorized 'playing,' in the same way as He did 'dividing,' and we refused to fellowship those who used instruments in the same way our 'one cup' brethren refuse to fellowship us, then the comparison would be valid. But He didn't. Those who add instruments are adding an element which is obviously, truly, never inferred or authorized in any New Testament text on the subject of music. However and quite to the contrary, in addition to noting the scripturally-provable 'dividing' of the fruit of the vine down among the disciples, we have also shown that in virtually every one of the thirty-one occurrences of the word "cup" in the New Testament – and even in those rare instances where a literal cup is there and in evidence - that it is also, somewhere in that same textual and contextual situation, used figuratively, metaphorically, or metonymically, to refer to or to symbolize something other than itself - and usually that was to refer to whatever the specific element or situation under consideration therein contained. A comparison of the eight New Testament texts in which the word "sing" occurs however, show no such thing.[65]

And finally, and in conclusion, when asked if there could be unity among 'one-cup' and 'multi-cup' congregations, his response was just another sad reminder of the ugly, gaping, and ungodly wound and division, which we are desperately in need of healing in the beloved and blood-bought body of Christ.

- *"We cannot have true unity with congregations that use instrumental music or individual cups in their worship services…*

The Conclusion Of The Whole Matter

Look; we all want the same exact thing here. I sincerely believe that every last one of us does – from the good sister who originally called the office from somewhere over closer to the east coast; to the 'one-cup' preaching brother over closer to the west coast; to myself and all of the faithful gospel preachers of the 'multi-cup' persuasion that I know; to the 'one-cup' brother whose interview we discussed in detail; and to each and every one of the sincerely God-seeking saints in the pews every Sunday on either side of this division. From everything I've ever read, seen, heard or studied from any of my brethren on either side of this division, I sincerely believe that we are all seeking exactly the same thing: to abide in God's word and thus know the truth that makes us free (John 8:31-32); to diligently study to present ourselves approved to God, as workers who do not need to be ashamed, rightly dividing the word of truth (2 Timothy 2:15); to faithfully worship in spirit

---

[65] "The Sin Of Offering Instrumental Music To God - Study And Worksheet.pdf," Douglas E. Dingley, accessed July 16, 2018, https://clevelandcofc.com/bible-studies/. (See it at: https://Godswordistruth.org/bible-studies/)

and truth and to thus be the kind of worshippers the Father is seeking (John 4:23-24); and to be faithful unto death that we might receive the crown of life (Revelation 2:10) and be gathered around His glorious throne forever together thereafter to worship the Lamb and Lord our God who is worthy (Revelation 5:6-14). I believe this is what all sincere New Testament Christians are truly seeking, wanting, and living, looking, and longing for.

It is these same sorts of sentiments that were also additionally reflected and expressed in the aforementioned and dissected interview and article as well; and these four additional comments by the way, with which I and so many of our 'multi-cup' brethren would also wholeheartedly agree (with but the one exception as addressed at the bottom of these four, following, additional excerpts from said interview):

- *"The proper observance of the Lord's Supper powerfully demonstrates our appreciation for both the love and lordship of Christ."*

- *"By faith, we obey the Lord regardless of the consequences (Hebrews 11:17-19, 24-27)."*

- *"Division in the body of Christ pains us. We deeply desire unity with all of our brothers and sisters, but truth comes before unity (John 17:17-21)."*

- *"We agree with brother McGarvey and plead with our dear brothers and sisters to carefully consider the grounds for unity on this issue."*

Obviously the one and only exception to any and all of our 'multi-cup' brethren's being in complete agreement with each and every word of our 'one-cup' brother's immediately above-stated comments, is the five-word portion relating to their agreeing with brother McGarvey. With all due respect, whether it is brother McGarvey, brother Woods, brother Campbell, brother Wade, brother Hickey, brother Dingley, or any other brother to have ever studied and taught the word of God, while it is wonderful, respectful, and often quite enlightening to examine their conclusions on any given topic, the 'bottom line' is that we must also, always, very objectively study, research, and compare their conclusions, to what the word of God says in all of its glorious and inerrant contextual purity, simplicity, totality, conclusions, references, inferences, figures of speech, and commandments; because truly, **truth must always come before, and therefore 'trump' unity with any human being's or preacher's conclusions, no matter what, or how well-loved, well-respected, or well-studied they may be (John 17:17-21).**

'Listen' brethren; if the Bereans were commended in the eternal text for daily and consistently, scripturally examining even the things taught by the divinely-inspired apostle Paul – and they were[66] – then we have no excuse for taking any human religious leader's word for anything – no matter how prominent he was, is, or how much he may have studied[67] – without making sure that we have first, thoroughly and completely tested and examined his words in the full light of the eternal word of the living God, to whom we shall all give an account (Romans 14:12). And that is precisely the process this book is intended to promote when it comes to the "cup."

Our 'one cup' brother asks in conclusion:

- *"What is the solution? Should those with Bible-based convictions shrug their shoulders and pretend nothing is wrong? Or should those who inherited the divisive practice from secular concerns rally to restore the intimacy that has been lost in communion and the unity that has been compromised within the body of Christ (1 Peter 2:17)?"*

His first two questions there are incredibly relevant, necessary, and desperately and definitely, deserve and demand, an accurate and biblical answer – which we shall provide momentarily. However, his final sentence just as desperately and definitely demands a well-deserved re-write. In light of all

---

[66] Acts 17:10-11.
[67] 1 Corinthians 1:10-13, 3:3-4.

we've studied throughout this book, that whole paragraph should be much more deservedly worded, asked, and answered thus:

> *"What is the solution? Should those with Bible-based convictions shrug their shoulders and pretend nothing is wrong?* NO! Absolutely not! That is the whole reason this book was written. This needless division has gone on for way, way, too long!
>
> *Or should those who insist on dividing the Lord's church by their binding where God has not bound due to their failure to differentiate and understand the difference between literal and figurative language rally to restore the intimacy that has been lost in communion and the unity that has been compromised within the body of Christ (1 Peter 2:17)?"* Yes! Absolutely! That is the whole reason this book was written! We need to restore the intimacy and unity that has been lost in the Lord's church, through the efforts of those brethren seeking to bind what God has not bound, and insisting that they cannot have fellowship with those who divide down the fruit of the vine before drinking it just exactly as Jesus commanded His disciples to do at the table that evening! We need to restore the spiritual intimacy and unity enjoyed by the first-century congregations as they all (even if eight days travel apart like Ephesus and Corinth) partook of the same cup of blessing! This needless division has gone on for far, far, too long!

You see, the real root of the division here is not whether a congregation uses one, or multiple communion cups. That's just the issue where the real problem manifests itself. Let me explain…

The Lord's word demands that His church assemble together for worship on the first day of the week.[68] But God has given us the personal and congregational freedom within that

---

[68] Acts 20:7-11.

divinely-directed and instituted "first day of the week" parameter, to decide for ourselves whether we will meet in a barn, church building, school building, private house, or wherever else; as well as exactly what hour, or hours, we will choose to meet. As long as we meet and carry out faithful to His word, spirit and truth worship according to His commandments during that first day of the week, the actual physical structure, lack thereof, or actual or literal hour or hours we as a congregation might choose to assemble together for worship do not matter to God. He gave us the freedom to decide those things from congregation to congregation, depending on our own particular circumstances.

The Lord's word also demands that His church sing Psalms, hymns, and spiritual songs to one another.[69] But God has given us the personal and congregational freedom within that divinely-directed and instituted "sing to one another" parameter, to decide for ourselves exactly which and how many Psalms, hymns, and spiritual songs we will choose to sing, as well as their order in the service, and/or whether we will sing them from memory, songbooks, or utilize a projection system. As long as we all sing and carry out faithful to His word, spirit and truth worship according to His commandments by singing, the actual songs, songbook colors, or whether or not we project the lyrics on a screen for all to follow does not matter to God. He gave us the freedom to decide those things from congregation to congregation. All that matters to Him is that we all sing to one another in accordance with His scriptural requirements.

While other examples could be cited, I think the point should be incredibly clear to all by now, as to how it relates to our current discussion and division. The Lord's word unquestionably and equilaterally demands that His church assemble together in small groups all over the globe to take communion every first day of the week just as we've previously and repeatedly seen evidenced. But within the parameters of that very divinely-directed and instituted "do this in remembrance of Me" event, God has given us certain personal and congregational freedoms to choose and decide for ourselves exactly how we're going to carry out that command.

---

[69] Ephesians 5:19; Colossians 3:16.

For example, it doesn't matter if the containers we use to carry out that command to partake are glass or plastic, wooden or ceramic, or square or cylindrical. All that matters to God is that all of His assembled children partake of the bread and fruit of the vine which symbolizes their unity and oneness in Christ and under His blood of the New Covenant. Now, if the congregation or congregational leadership in a particular location decides that they are going to use only one cup instead of multiple cups to carry that out that commandment, good for them! No problem. May God bless them as they do so!

On the other hand, if the congregation or congregational leadership in another location decides that they are going to use multiple cups instead of one cup to carry that out (dividing down the fruit of the vine amongst themselves before drinking *it* just as we see Jesus' disciples being told to do in Luke 22:17-20), good for them! No problem. May God bless them as they do so. What matters to God is that we all humbly, submissively, reverently and obediently partake of those same, two, exclusive elements – the bread and the fruit of the vine – which make us all spiritually one as we do so. Period.

But where the real root of the problem comes from, is the same source from whence the very similar problem came for the first-century congregation in Antioch and those of the surrounding Galatian region. As you will readily recall, the problem which the apostle Paul had to address there that was similarly causing strife, division, chaos and confusion amongst the brethren, and which was the same, exact, colossal and widespread problem that necessitated the so-called Acts Fifteen Jerusalem Conference was this:

There were certain zealously religious people, who were militantly and aggressively insisting on binding a practice on the church members, which God had not, in any way, shape, or form, bound on them!

Their message as they sought to insist on going beyond what was written[70] and binding where God had not bound? If I may paraphrase: 'Do this… or else!'[71] Sound familiar? And just as faithful, first-century church leaders such as Paul, Barnabas, and the other apostles and elders met, discussed, and decided to make sure that such binding where God had not bound was not going to be allowed to stand back then, so too, must faithful church leadership today, stand against and opposed to all such binding where God has not bound, just as strongly and adamantly as they also stand up against any and all unbinding what God has bound.

Do you perhaps additionally also recall the divinely-inspired apostle Paul's response to those zealous but zealously misled religious folks in Galatians, Chapter Five? And just how fitting and applicable for our current division are his words which follow those first dozen verses? "For you, brethren, have been called to liberty; only do not *use* liberty as an opportunity for the flesh, but through love serve one another. For all the law is fulfilled in one word, *even* in this: *'You shall love your neighbor as yourself.'* But if you bite and devour one another, beware lest you be consumed by one another" (Galatians 5:13-15). Biting, devouring, and condemning brethren just because they understand the difference between figurative and literal language and when God has allowed them certain freedoms insofar as how to carry out certain of His commandments, instead of allowing themselves to be bound up in those man-made laws and bonds insisted upon by some religious zealots who would bind where God has not, is definitely a sin which is highly offensive to God according to these verses, is it not?

As a fellow preacher and brother of the 'Non-Institutional' persuasion one state away once stated to me in an e-mail: "*Always remember: 'When a man/woman who is honestly mistaken hears the truth, he/she will either quit being mistaken, or cease to be honest.'*" I couldn't agree with him more. I hope and pray that this book will eventually be 'poured over' with a

---

[70] 1 Corinthians 4:6: (Please note: it is also very interesting when one examines this actual verse in Scripture, to see that the apostle Paul verified that he also taught using figurative language and applications as opposed to always speaking in literal terms.)
[71] Acts 15:1.

'fine tooth comb' by each and every one of my beloved, and hopefully honestly mistaken brethren of the 'one cup' persuasion, and that its contents will be meticulously studied, and honestly, objectively, and sincerely compared to Scripture, in order to validate that the things herein stated are true.

But what if some continue to insist on an absolutely, no exceptions insistence on only and exclusively 'one cup' in communion... *or else*? What about those who might seek to continue to carry this division-causing and caustic doctrine forward by continuing to seek to try to bind that – one, lone, literal, physical cup for communion (a practice which even they themselves, in reality are not able to carry out) - which God has not bound, and thus further seek to condemn and alienate their beloved and blood-bought brethren who simply seek to faithfully follow what their Lord instituted in Luke 22:17-20, along with Matthew 26:26-29 and Mark 14:22-25? Well, as to God's response, I'll leave that up to Him.

As to our response however, please let me first say that I hope you noticed that throughout this book I have repeatedly referred to these brethren as exactly what they are: "brethren." Yours and mine. It is not those of us who understand the difference between when the Lord is using figurative as opposed to literal language; who are obediently submitting to the Lord who told His disciples to divide the fruit of the vine among themselves before drinking it; and who understand that we have the freedom to use as few or as many containers as we see fit to faithfully and expediently carry out that commandment; who are drawing the lines of division between ourselves and others of our blood bought brethren over their same divinely-instituted freedom to expediently choose as well, within the absolute parameters our almighty God has laid down. However, as brethren faithfully following our Lord's instructions, may I also say that we would be left with no other biblical option at the point - should some of our 'one-cup' brethren choose to continue to persist in binding where God did not bind - but to faithfully obey our Lord's instructions from Romans 16:17-18, 2 John 9-11, and similar others as well.

But, I certainly hope that such is not the case that we have to go that far. I hope and pray that all will instead, seek to be the answer to Jesus' prayer for oneness as He prayed the night before His crucifixion for us, as recorded in John 17:20-23. I hope and pray that all will instead follow the apostle Paul's divinely-inspired instructions to our beloved and blood-bought brethren in first-century Ephesus: "I, therefore, the prisoner of the Lord, beseech you to walk worthy of the calling with which you were called, with all lowliness and gentleness, with longsuffering, bearing with one another in love, endeavoring to keep the unity of the Spirit in the bond of peace" (Ephesians 4:1-3). I hope and pray that our 'one-cup' brethren, will one day soon, simply be happy and content, to simply be our "brethren," and once again work together in good and faithful fellowship with us, as we are all essential and much-needed and necessary members of the body of Christ[72], period.

If I might now conclude, with basically the same sentiments which concluded Chapter Three:

Can you even begin to imagine the invincible force for Christ that we could truly become in our lost world today, were we all but to completely humble ourselves before God, get on the same spiritual page, teach the same divinely-inspired doctrine, and become the one, same, united and unified church and answer to Jesus' prayer which He prayed we'd be the very night before He was crucified (John 17:20-23; 1 Corinthians 4:17, 7:17, 11:16, 16:1-2)? Wouldn't it be wonderful to help steer toward the day when a new *Churches of Christ in the United States* directory could be published, 'wherein there was neither one cup nor non-institutional, no no-class nor instrumental, nor male or female pride and power driven agendas, but that we were all truly one in Christ Jesus? Brethren, let's answer our Lord's prayer, YES!

---

[72] 1 Corinthians 12:12-27.

Chapter Twelve:

The Crusade
(Epilogue)

June 1, 2000 was the opening evening of the third and final Billy Graham Crusade in Nashville, Tennessee. That evening, preaching students from the *Memphis School of Preaching*, as well as brother Garland Elkins[73] who coordinated the effort, along with a few other folks, helped to distribute thousands of teaching brochures on the sidewalks leading to the stadium. The tract that they distributed that evening was one written by brothers Garland Elkins and James McGill, entitled, *"Baptism: The Bible and Billy Graham."* The contents of that tract are reprinted below.[74]

As Billy Graham closes his sermons, he often tells his hearers that there are three things they must do:

(1) Repent

Graham then gives a good definition of repentance. This requirement is biblical. On the day the church began almost two thousand years ago, when the apostles preached the first gospel sermon, thousands in their hearing *"were pricked in their heart."* They asked Peter and the other apostles what they should do.

---

[73] "Remembering Garland Elkins," The Gospel Gleaner, Jim McGill, http://gospelgleaner.com/?page_id=894.
[74] Reprinted with permission from brother James McGill and sister Corinne Elkins.

Then Peter said unto them, Repent, and be baptized every one of you in the name of Jesus Christ for the remission of your sins, and ye shall receive the gift of the Holy Ghost (Acts 2:38).

(2) Believe

Graham stresses that this faith means total trust in Jesus – not just a mere intellectual act of mental asset. Again, Billy Graham is Biblical in saying belief is necessary. Jesus said, in giving what is often called the Great Commission:

"He that believeth and is baptized shall be saved…" (Mark 16:16)

(3) Live For Jesus

There are many New Testament Scriptures that command this. See, for example, Second Peter 1:5-11.

Billy Graham has consistently named these three things that every accountable person must do to be saved. He has preached this message to countless millions in crusades, over radio, on television, in newspaper articles, and in books, for more than half a century. Among his numerous best-selling books, Billy Graham wrote one entitled **How To Be Born Again**.

Graham is exactly right in saying all three of the commands must be obeyed. **(1) Repent, (2) Believe, and (3) Live for Jesus.** (We may wonder why he places repentance before faith. In the recorded instances of conversion from the time the church began, in the New Testament Book of Acts, it was faith that came first and that motivated and led to the additional acts of obedience.)

But There Are More Than Just Three Steps In God's Plan Of Salvation.

To **leave out even one step** changes the gospel. It changes the plan of salvation just as surely as *adding* an unauthorized act would change God's plan. Compare Galatians 1:6-10.

Suppose we are giving someone directions to a certain destination. And suppose there are *four* turns he must make. We must tell him correctly about all four turns. If we neglect to mention any turn – just one turn – then that person would not get to his destination.

For half a century Billy Graham has consistently failed to include **baptism** when he tells those seeking salvation what they must do to be saved! Billy Graham has been reading from the Scriptures and using passages from the Bible in his preaching for more than fifty years. Now, the most puzzling question ever:

How Could Billy Graham Have Failed To See In The Bible The Command To Be Baptized For The Remission Of Sins?

Billy Graham readily sees the command to believe in Mark 16:16: *"He that believeth and is baptized shall be saved..."* He clearly sees the commandment to repent in Acts 2:38: *"Repent and be baptized every one of you in the name of Jesus Christ, for the remission of sins..."*

Yet somehow, incredible as it seems, he has never seen Jesus' command to be baptized to *"be saved"* (Mark 16:16) or the command to *"be baptized... for the remission of sins"* (Acts 2:38).

Seemingly, all through the years, Billy Graham has looked at these Bible verses as though they read... *"He that believeth --- shall be saved"* (Mark 16:16) and *"Repent --- every one of you in the name of Jesus Christ, for the remission of sins"* (Acts 2:38).

How could Billy Graham have failed to see Jesus' words **"and is baptized"** in Mark 16:16? How could Billy Graham have overlooked Peter's words **"and be baptized"** in Acts 2:38?

An Old Question

This is not a new question. About fifty years ago, during the Billy Graham month-long Crusade in Nashville at the Vanderbilt University football stadium, someone asked a member of the *Billy Graham Evangelistic Association* team this question directly:

**"Why does Billy Graham
not include the command to be baptized
in his preaching?"**

The short and very unsatisfactory answer was: **"Because it is
a controversial subject."**

A further insight into this strange phenomenon came to light a few years later with the publication of Leslie L. Spear's book *The True Religion and Religion of Others*. When that book was published, one chapter attracted immediate attention, and created intense interest: **Chapter 2** – an exchange of letters between the author and the *Billy*

Graham Evangelistic Association in Minneapolis.

The first letter, dated January 12, 1963, was written by Leslie L. Spear from Oak Ridge, Tennessee, in response to a Billy Graham *My Answer* column that had just appeared in the *Knoxville Journal.* An inquirer had asked Billy Graham: "Please give me a simple answer to '**What must I do to be saved?**'" Billy Graham completely failed to mention **baptism** in his reply!

In Leslie Spear's letter to Billy Graham, he quoted the words of Jesus: *"He that believeth and is baptized shall be saved..."* (Mark 16:16). Spear says that Graham might have included *that* Scripture as part of an appropriate answer to the question.

Spear then quotes the words of Paul the apostle in Galatians 3:27: *"For as many of you as have been baptized into Christ have put on Christ."* At this point in his letter, Leslie Spear puts his first direct question to Billy Graham:

> *"Mr. Graham, why didn't you give Paul's answer to the question? You could have told where it was found, so the person could have read it for himself."*

On April 17, 1963, Leslie Spear received a reply from the *Billy Graham Evangelistic Association.* It was signed by John D. Lundenburg, Spiritual Counselor. At last, there was to be an answer to this puzzling question! But the part of the answer that responds directly to the question is brief:

> *"Salvation is not dependent upon a person having been baptized..."*

There it is! When people have been steeped in centuries of religious prejudice, they can somehow read right through all the Scriptures that teach clearly that obedience in baptism **is** necessary for salvation.

The doctrine that salvation can occur before and without baptism for the remission of sins has been preached millions of times since it first began to be taught in Europe five centuries ago.

That doctrine has been repeated so many times that even otherwise able men like Billy Graham have been saturated with it. **They** were taught the doctrine just as if it were true – even Biblical! Yet, to say that obedience in baptism is not necessary for salvation is just as false as it was when men like John Calvin invented and propagated the doctrine in the 1500's.[75]

The Result

Think of the multiplied millions who have heard and accepted Billy Graham's teaching. Every one of these souls will one day stand before God in the Great Day of Judgment. They will not be able to account for why they were not baptized for the forgiveness of their sins – except to say, honestly, *"Billy Graham didn't tell me I had to do that!"*

And Billy Graham will face God in judgment, too, as all people – great and small – must do. What will he answer if God asks, **"Billy, why did you never tell all these millions that they must be baptized to be saved?"**

---

[75] "2 Church Histories & The Origin Of The So-Called 'Sinner's Prayer'.pdf," Douglas E. Dingley, accessed July 16, 2018, https://clevelandcofc.com/bible-studies/. (See it at: https://Godswordistruth.org/bible-studies/)

> *"...be baptized, and wash away thy sins..."*
> *~Acts 22:16*

> *"...baptism doth also now save us..."*
> *~First Peter 3:21*

As one final footnote to this false, fatal, and fallacious doctrine of salvation occurring before and without baptism, and the fact that it is still taught and defended by Graham's followers and association, a post at www.billygraham.org seeking to address the question, "Is baptism essential for salvation?" is answered thus:

> "To one who has received Christ, baptism is a necessary and meaningful experience... You may know that we urge immediate and extensive Bible study for each convert. As the Scripture is reviewed, the place of baptism will surely be discovered. If baptism were a requirement for salvation, we would certainly say that. But you couldn't support that, knowing, for example, that the thief on the cross had no opportunity for baptism or church membership."

And as we know, this response shows a total and undeniable lack of biblical knowledge, understanding, or acknowledgment of the fact, that of course the thief on the cross didn't have to be baptized to be saved, **_because He lived and died under the Old Covenant!_** This Grahamatic answer utterly and completely fails to take into account and apply such vital passages as Galatians 4:1-7 and Hebrews 9:15-17 to the overall New Testament salvation 'portrait' that God 'paints' for us in the sacred text! So of course it's going to be an erroneous answer; because those furnishing it fail to take into account **_all_** of the relevant verses on the subject, or their context and connection to said topic! They sincerely believe that they're giving folks the full picture, but without their having put all the 'pieces of the puzzle' properly in place to begin with! Hence the 'holes' in their answer! Such "Scripture-plucking" always leads to just such error, confusion, and eventually, if not corrected, spiritual death and destruction. Of course, the thief on the cross did not need to be baptized in order to be saved and had no opportunity for church membership - BECAUSE THE NEW COVENANT/ TESTAMENT HADN'T COME INTO EFFECT YET, AND THE LORD'S ONE NEW TESTAMENT CHURCH HADN'T BEEN ESTABLISHED YET! That crowning achievement of God's plan[76] would come about and into existence some fifty days later, and only after the thief's death.[77]

So, why is all of this information presented in the epilogue of a book on the topic of communion cups? Simple. Because the comparisons are stunningly striking! For example:

- I wonder how many souls might possibly be lost because they chose to trust their salvation to some of the brethren of the 'one cup only or else' insistence, simply because they had written several books or had their own television shows, instead of truly praying[78], studying[79], and 'pouring over' all of the relevant verses on the subject within God's word for themselves (such as have been laboriously examined herein)?

- Because it is still true that people who have been steeped in years of religious prejudice can, easily, if they are not careful, read right through all of the Scriptures that prove that the 'one cup only or else' doctrine has gaping 'holes' in it rendering it biblically unsustainable and 'unable to hold water,' and yet, still seek to defend it.

- And as we know, that 'one cup only or else' doctrine, too, has been repeated so many times that in some cases, even otherwise able brethren have been 'saturated' with it. ***They*** were taught the doctrine just as if it were true – even Biblical! Think of the multiplied thousands who have heard and accepted it. And yet, when we add all of the verses together – i.e., when we add Luke's account

---

[76] See Ephesians 3:8-12.
[77] Acts 2:1-47.
[78] James 1:5-8.
[79] 2 Timothy 2:15-16; 2 Peter 1:20-2:3, 3:17-18.

to both Matthew and Mark's – we see the whole 'picture' of Jesus' disciples dividing and then drinking the fruit of the vine that pre-crucifixion evening, become much clearer indeed. Do you see it yet? In fact, that scriptural picture is so incredibly clear that we dare not tamper with nor distort it in any way (2 Corinthians 4:2).

As you prepare to close out this study, please understand what is at stake. This is about far, far, infinitely more than just the number of communion containers a particular congregation chooses to utilize in their weekly celebration of the Lord's communion. It is about rightly dividing, contextually understanding, properly applying, and humbly obeying the entire word of God (Matthew 4:4), fitted perfectly together in all of its individual as well as consummate and incredible eternal glory (Psalm 119:160). Because when even the best of intentioned and most religiously-zealous of brethren do not do these things, and then, additionally insist on enforcing their own imperfect and erroneously-arrived at conclusions on the entire blood-bought brotherhood of our Lord and Savior Jesus Christ... countless, precious, and priceless eternal souls are at stake – and Satan is ecstatic.

Never forget exactly how Satan works and what his first, greatest, and most powerful deception consisted of: Tying a deadly and deceptive "not" into the very fabric of God's divine and life-giving commandment, which completely reversed, negated, and contradicted God's commandment and the good and godly intention behind it. This then cost those who had been walking with Him to that point, both their pure and perfect relationship with God, as well as their life in His presence and the paradise which accompanied it. And I believe the very essence of the 'one cup or else' insistence can all be 'boiled down' to that one, same, soul-condemning and commandment-contradicting reversive reasoning of Satan. For in its purest, simplest, and most basic fallacious form, this 'one cup or else' doctrine:

Requires the keeping together as one, that which the Lord commanded His disciples to divide down (Luke 22:17); while subsequently demanding the dividing down, of that

which our Lord desired His disciples to preserve and keep together as one (John 17:20-22; Ephesians 4:1-6).

Brethren, we cannot afford to let Satan win this one. The beautiful, beloved, and blood-bought bride of our Lord Jesus Christ has been needlessly and painfully suffering through this ugly, ghastly, and ungodly wound and division for far, far too long already. We have the remedy. We know the cure. Let's put an end to her hurting, pain, and suffering, while initiating her healing in our generation. This, by thus coming and standing together just as our loving Lord and Savior instructed, in a thorough and well-studied, in-common and contextual understanding and practice of the communion celebration which makes us all one, as we partake of the bread and the fruit of the vine in humble, obedient, and well-informed and biblical compliance with our Lord's commandments each and every Lord's Day, no matter where we are the world over, just as the first century church of our Lord Jesus Christ did as well. God bless!

Appendix Study
(From Chapter 3)

The entire mindset behind the whole "Non-Institutional" or "Anti-istic" approach to and perspective on Scripture, seems to be summed up in brother Robby Eversole's words from ***"Polishing The Pulpit"*** as seen quoted in Chapter Three: *"Anti's take one way you can do something, and make it the ONLY way it can be done – or else..."* Not only should the fallacy of such an approach be instantly obvious, but one possible reason for such an approach might also be just as obvious, and just as quickly and easily addressed as well. Consider...

There are some truths in the Bible that are most certainly, assuredly, absolutely and exclusively, "one way." There are no other options, exceptions, exclusions, or freedoms to deviate even the least iota, in any direction whatsoever, without incurring the rightful and holy wrath of almighty God.

Such "one way" and "one way only" God-given truths would include such things as the fact that Jesus Christ is the one, lone, only and exclusive way to heaven - no matter what – and that there is just no other way there whatsoever, except through Him (John 14:6). Period.

The "seven ones" of Ephesians 4:4-6 are just as "one and only one" exclusive and prohibitive. There simply is no other option, other than the one, lone, God-given and God approved and documented "one body" (or church – Ephesians 1:22-23), "one Lord," "one faith," "one baptism," and etc., other than and aside from the "one" that is mentioned therein. Period.

And so the question now becomes: "Have we really spent so much time in defending the exclusivity of such God-given and definitive 'ones' to our denominational friends and family, that we somehow no longer know how to understand, process, accept and implement those truths wherein God has given us more than one option or command?" For example, what did the first-century church do when they met on the first day of the week? They broke bread (Acts 20:7). But they also gave of their means (1 Corinthians 16:1-2). Therefore, to insist that either one of those acts of worship is the only and exclusive one we are commanded to perform on the first day of the week – to the complete and utter exclusion of the other one – would be spiritually suicidal, would it not? Yes, it would (John 10:35). But what if someone then went even further, so much so as to insist that anyone following what God said to do on the first day of the week in the other passage was going to hell for so doing?

Additionally, we have examples in Scripture of praying being done both on a mountain at night (Luke 6:12), as well as in a garden at night (Luke 22:39-46); of God's people praying in an upper room (Acts 1:12-14), as well as heading up to the temple to pray in the afternoon (Acts 3:1); of a regular place of prayer being on the banks of a river (Acts 16:13), as well as His people praying at midnight in prison (Acts 16:25); of being instructed to pray before meals (1 Timothy 4:4-5), as well as at various and assorted other times and locations. We also see several different postures and 'positions' of prayer recorded in Scripture as well (1 Kings 8:22, 54, 19:4; 2 Kings 20:1-3; Daniel 6:10; Jonah 2:1; Matthew 26:39; Mark 14:35; Acts 9:40, 20:36, 21:5; 1 Timothy 2:8; and etc.). So; which one, lone, exclusive, particular time, location, and posture of prayer is the absolutely only one which is acceptable to God? Answer (obviously): Not one, but all of the above.

Surely all can see the spiritual danger inherent in taking just one of the multiple ways God's word says we can do something in those instances wherein He has given us several different options, and then seeking to insist on making it the ONLY way it can be done – or else. (And incidentally, what would make that any different or more noble than doing the exact opposite, by taking the one and only way God said something was to be done and then diversifying and doing that in a variety of completely different ways from what He said?)

Surely, we can all also agree that many of our lost denominational friends and family have done a very similar thing when it comes to something as all-important as their salvation. They have taken only the verses that connect "belief" to salvation (such as John 3:16), to the complete and total exclusion of all of the biblical verses which just as correctly connect "baptism" to said salvation (such as Acts 2:38, 22:16; 1 Peter 3:21 and so many others), and have therefore built what is a very fatal, faulty, and erroneous theology of salvation, upon what boils down to nothing more than very spiritually weak and shifting sand (Matthew 7:21-27).

Let us all determine to study the Scriptures daily, in order to differentiate between when God is giving us the one and only exclusive way in which He wants something done… and when He is giving us only one of several different and divinely-inspired options in a given text… And may we never cross or confuse the two.

PHOTOS

[i] John Snyder, Lord's cup and bread and bible, 2013, photograph, https://commons.wikimedia.org/wiki/File:Bible_and_Lord%27s_Cup_and_Bread.JPG (use of this photographer's work does not suggest that they endorse the author or his work).
[ii] JKP, 2018, photograph.
[iii] https://www.soonereastcofc.com/about-us, photograph.

Scan with Your Phone to Go To These Links

http://www.jameskaypublishing.com/BookStore.html

www.amazon.com/author/douglasdingley

http://churchofchristarticles.com/blog/category/doug-dingley

https://Godswordistruth.org/bible-studies/

https://Godswordistruth.org/sermons/

www.ingramcontent.com/pod-product-compliance
Lightning Source LLC
Chambersburg PA
CBHW060827050426
42453CB00008B/617